Domain-Driven Design

Use Golang to create simple, maintainable systems to solve complex business problems

Matthew Boyle

BIRMINGHAM—MUMBAI

Domain-Driven Design with Golang

Group Product Manager: Gebin George
Publishing Product Manager: Pooja Yadav
Senior Editor: Kinnari Chohan
Technical Editor: Pradeep Sahu
Copy Editor: Safis Editing
Project Coordinator: Deeksha Thakkar
Proofreader: Safis Editing
Indexer: Subalakshmi Govindhan
Production Designer: Aparna Bhagat
Developer Relations Marketing Executive: Sonakshi Bubbar
Technical Reviewers: Andrea Medda, Matthew Williams, Chris Shepherd

First published: December 2022

Production reference: 2141222

Published by Packt Publishing Ltd.
Livery Place
35 Livery Street
Birmingham
B3 2PB, UK.

ISBN 978-1-80461-345-0

www.packt.com

To my partner Hannah, who is always supportive of my schemes, no matter how ludicrous (writing this book being one of my wilder ones).

To the memory of my mother Sarah, whom I miss every day and I'm certain would have displayed this book proudly (but never have read it).

Contributors

About the author

Matthew Boyle is an experienced technical leader in the field of distributed systems, specializing in using Go. He has worked at huge companies such as Cloudflare and General Electric, as well as exciting high-growth startups such as Curve and Crowdcube. Matt has been writing Go for production since 2018 and often shares blog posts and fun trivia about Go over on Twitter (@MattJamesBoyle).

Andrea Medda is an experienced Go engineer from Sardinia. Andrea has a strong interest in clean, maintainable code that scales.

About the reviewers

Matthew Williams is a (mainly) backend Software Engineer generally working in Java or Kotlin, who has dabbled in Go. Regardless of the language used, he is a proponent of Domain-Driven Design, Test-Driven Development and occasionally, Frustration-Driven Development. Originally a University of Birmingham Computer Science classmate of the author, he has spent time working across both the public and private sectors in the UK and Australia. Working for the likes of the Science and Technology Facilities Council, SAP, and Tyro on domains including scientific research proposals, e-commerce, and payments, the need to understand and use the language of the domain has always been clear.

Chris Shepherd is currently employed as a Systems Engineer building large scale, highly-available and robust distributed systems. He has worked within software engineering for more than seven years, the majority of which have been dedicated to writing Go. He has worked for both big-name companies, such as IBM and Cloudflare, and fast paced, hyper-growth startups, spanning across many different industries, including finance, cybersecurity, and the public sector. He received a BSc in Computer Science from De Montfort University and is currently employed by Cloudflare, where he designs, develops, and maintains highly scalable event-driven microservices in Go.

Table of Contents

Preface   ix

Part 1: Introduction to Domain-Driven Design

1

A Brief History of Domain-Driven Design   3

The world before DDD   3   Adoption of DDD   7
So, what are OOD patterns?   5   When should you use DDD?   9
Eric Evans and DDD   6   Summary   10
Three pillars of DDD   6   Further reading   11

2

Understanding Domains, Ubiquitous Language, and Bounded Contexts   13

Technical requirements   13   Bounded contexts   21
Setting the scene   14   Open Host Service   22
Domains and sub-domains   16   Published language   24
Ubiquitous language   16   Anti-corruption layer   36
Benefits of ubiquitous language   17   Summary   38
                                            Further reading   39

3

Entities, Value Objects, and Aggregates   41

Technical requirements   42   The aggregate pattern   53
Working with entities   42   Discovering aggregates   55
Generating good identifiers   44   Designing aggregates   56
A warning when defining entities   45   Aggregates beyond a single bounded context   57
A note on object-relational mapping   49
                                                Summary   57
Working with value objects   49   Further reading   57
How should I decide whether to use an entity
or value object?   53

4

Exploring Factories, Repositories, and Services   59

Technical requirements   59   Understanding services   66
Introducing the factory pattern   60   Domain services   66
Entity factories   63   Application services   69
Implementing the repository pattern   Summary   75
in Golang   63

Part 2: Real -World Domain-Driven Design with Golang

5

Applying DDD to a Monolithic Application   79

Technical requirements   79   Adding an infrastructure service for payment
What do we mean when we say   handling   96
monolithic application?   80   Paying with CoffeeBux   98
Setting the scene   81   Adding store-specific discounts 102
Getting started with our CoffeeCo   Extending our service   108
system   83   Summary   109
Implementing our product repository   93   Further reading   109

6

Building a Microservice Using DDD   111

Technical requirements   111
A friendly warning (again)   112
What do we mean by microservices?   112
What are the benefits of microservices?   113
What are the downsides of microservices?   113
Should my company adopt
microservices?   114

Setting the scene (again)   114
Building a recommendation system   116
Revisiting the anti-corruption layer   121
Exposing our service via an open
host service   124
Summary   131

7

DDD for Distributed Systems   133

Technical requirements   133
What is a distributed system?   134
CAP theorem and databases   135
Distributed system patterns   137
CQRS   137
EDA   139
Dealing with failure   141
Two-phase commit (2PC)   141

The saga pattern   142
What is a message bus?   145
Kafka   145
RabbitMQ   146
NATS   148
Summary   149
Further reading   149

8

TDD, BDD, and DDD   151

Technical requirements   151
TDD   152
Adding a test   154
Run the test we just wrote – it should fail (and
we should expect it to)   155

Write as little code as possible to pass the test   156
Refactoring   162
BDD   174
Summary   177

Index   179

Other Books You May Enjoy   184

Preface

Welcome to this book on Domain-driven design with Golang!

DDD is one of the most sought-after skills in the industry. This book provides you with step-by-step explanations of essential concepts, and practical examples that will see you introducing DDD in your Go projects in no time.

Domain-Driven Design with Golang starts by helping you gain a basic understanding of DDD, and then covers all the important patterns such as bounded contexts, Ubiquitous Language, aggregates, and more. The latter half of this book deals with the real-world implementation of Domain-driven design patterns, and teaches you to build two systems whilst applying DDD principles, which will be a valuable addition to your portfolio. Finally, you'll find out how to build a microservice, along with learning how DDD-based microservices can be part of a greater distributed system.

Although the focus of this book is Golang, by the end of this book, you'll be able to confidently use DDD patterns outside of Go and apply them to other languages and even distributed systems.

Who this book is for

This book is intended for intermediate Go developers who are looking to take their enterprise skills to the next level, however, I really hope I have made it accessible enough that beginners can follow along too.

If you have never written Go before, but have some familiarity with DDD, I hope this book will help you use your expertise to write Domain-driven Go in an idiomatic way.

Finally, if you are an expert in DDD and in Golang, I hope this book serves as a great reference that you can pick up from time to time when you can't quite remember something.

What this book covers

Chapter 1, A Brief History of Domain-Driven Design helps you learn about the origins of DDD – no Golang in this chapter!

Chapter 2, Understanding Domains, Ubiquitous Language, and Bounded Contexts teaches you these core domain-driven topics.

Chapter 3, Entities, Value Objects, and Aggregates will help you learn a few more DDD topics.

Chapter 4, Exploring Factories, Repositories, and Services is the final chapter of Part 1, and sees us learn three more DDD patterns that will help cement our understanding.

Chapter 5, Applying DDD to a Monolithic Application teaches how we can apply domain-driven design to both an existing monolithic application, but also to a new one we will build together.

Chapter 6, Building a Microservice using DDD shows how to build a microservice using DDD that is resilient to failure.

Chapter 7, DDD for Distributed Systems takes you through how DDD can be applied to entire distributed systems as well as covering topics such as message queues at a foundational level.

Chapter 8, TDD, BDD and BDD is a bonus chapter that covers how test-driven development, behaviour-driven development, and domain-driven development can be complimentary patterns.

To get the most out of this book

Software/hardware covered in the book	Operating system requirements
Go 1.19.3 or above	Windows, macOS, or Linux
VS Code or Goland	
Docker	

If you are using the digital version of this book, we advise you to type the code yourself or access the code from the book's GitHub repository (a link is available in the next section). Doing so will help you avoid any potential errors related to the copying and pasting of code.

Download the example code files

You can download the example code files for this book from GitHub at `https://github.com/PacktPublishing/Domain-Driven-Design-with-GoLang`. If there's an update to the code, it will be updated in the GitHub repository.

We also have other code bundles from our rich catalog of books and videos available at `https://github.com/PacktPublishing/`. Check them out!

Download the color images

We also provide a PDF file that has color images of the screenshots and diagrams used in this book. You can download it here: `https://packt.link/1Xo4T`.

Conventions used

There are a number of text conventions used throughout this book.

`Code in text`: Indicates code words in text, database table names, folder names, filenames, file extensions, pathnames, dummy URLs, user input, and Twitter handles. Here is an example: "Firstly, we will define a `Point` in the following code block."

A block of code is set as follows:

```
=== RUN Test_Point
value_objects_test.go:13: a and b were not equal
--- FAIL: Test_Point (0.00s)
```

> **Tips or important notes**
> Appear like this.

Get in touch

Feedback from our readers is always welcome.

General feedback: If you have questions about any aspect of this book, email us at customercare@packtpub.com and mention the book title in the subject of your message.

Errata: Although we have taken every care to ensure the accuracy of our content, mistakes do happen. If you have found a mistake in this book, we would be grateful if you would report this to us. Please visit www.packtpub.com/support/errata and fill in the form.

Piracy: If you come across any illegal copies of our works in any form on the internet, we would be grateful if you would provide us with the location address or website name. Please contact us at copyright@packt.com with a link to the material.

If you are interested in becoming an author: If there is a topic that you have expertise in and you are interested in either writing or contributing to a book, please visit authors.packtpub.com.

Share Your Thoughts

Once you've read *Domain-Driven Design with Golang*, we'd love to hear your thoughts! Scan the QR code below to go straight to the Amazon review page for this book and share your feedback.

https://packt.link/r/1804613452

Your review is important to us and the tech community and will help us make sure we're delivering excellent quality content.

Download a free PDF copy of this book

Thanks for purchasing this book!

Do you like to read on the go but are unable to carry your print books everywhere?

Is your eBook purchase not compatible with the device of your choice?

Don't worry, now with every Packt book you get a DRM-free PDF version of that book at no cost.

Read anywhere, any place, on any device. Search, copy, and paste code from your favorite technical books directly into your application.

The perks don't stop there, you can get exclusive access to discounts, newsletters, and great free content in your inbox daily

Follow these simple steps to get the benefits:

1. Scan the QR code or visit the link below

https://packt.link/free-ebook/9781804613450

2. Submit your proof of purchase

3. That's it! We'll send your free PDF and other benefits to your email directly

Part 1:
Introduction to
Domain-Driven Design

Part 1 of *Domain-driven design with Golang* focuses on ensuring you are familiar with the core DDD concepts. We start by exploring the history of DDD, as I truly believe that context is important when applying software patterns. We then move on to exploring each DDD concept in isolation by firstly learning the theory behind them and then applying them with Golang code. This lays a great foundation for *Part 2*, where we will build two projects from scratch and use all the DDD concepts we learnt in this first part.

This part comprises the following chapters:

- *Chapter 1, A Brief History of DDD*
- *Chapter 2, Understanding Domains, Ubiquitous Language, and Bounded Contexts*
- *Chapter 3, Entities, Value Objects, and Aggregates*
- *Chapter 4, Factories, Repositories, and Services*

1

A Brief History of
Domain-Driven Design

Welcome to this book on **domain-driven design** (DDD) using **Golang**. If you have never heard of DDD before, I hope that by the end of this book, you will have a good understanding of what it is, where it came from, how it can be applied, and how to implement some of the patterns popular among DDD proponents using Golang.

You might be surprised to discover that a large part of the first half of this book will be defining terms and discussing patterns on how to work with others to build systems that represent the real world. At its core, this is what DDD is about. Don't worry though; there will be plenty of Golang examples, and in *Part 2*, we will dive deeper into building out DDD-based systems.

In this chapter, we will explore how DDD emerged and gained popularity. I find this context particularly valuable as we delve deeper into the topic as it helps you understand *why* to use it, not just *how*.

In this chapter, we will cover the following topics:

- The world before DDD
- Eric Evans and DDD
- Three pillars of DDD
- Adoption of DDD
- When should you use DDD?

The world before DDD

Before 2003 and the inception of DDD, engineers and architects were thinking about how to organize their software and systems in a way that represented the problem space (domain) they were trying to model. As software became more and more complicated, it became apparent that the closer your system was to the domain, the easier it was to make changes. More importantly, it was easier for other stakeholders to converse with engineers as there was less of a disconnect between the real-world model of the problem space and the system model.

This was the issue that Eric Evans, a software engineer, was facing—the increased complexity of systems and failures in creating and maintaining them. This led him to write the book *Domain-Driven Design: Tackling Complexity in the Heart of Software*, Addison-Wesley Professional, in 2003—the first book on the subject of DDD.

"...(The) book Domain-Driven Design was an attempt to capture for people the successful practices that I had seen or used, some of which have been around for a long time and some of which are relatively new, and put together into a coherent set of practices with clear names so that maybe we can have broader success than we have in the past... a great deal of domain-driven design comes straight out of good old-fashioned object-oriented design patterns." (Evans, in an interview with *Software Engineering Radio*, 2019, *Episode 8*: https://youtu.be/7yUONWp-CxM)

What does Evans mean when he refers to **object-oriented design (OOD)** principles? It used to be a given that everyone would write some **object-oriented (OO)** code as they began their journey into software development, but that is not necessarily the case anymore. If you are reading this book and Golang is your first programming language, it might be that you have never written traditional OO code.

OO programming (OOP) is a way to write programs that allows us to organize our code around objects rather than functions. We give these objects attributes and methods that define behavior.

OOP is particularly popular for large complex code bases as OOP is much easier to reason about. One of the most popular OOP languages is **Java**.

If we were building a **human resources (HR)** system, we might want to model an employee. If we were using Java, we might write this as follows:

```java
public class Employee {

    private String firstName;
    private String lastName;

    public Employee (String firstName, String lastName) {
        this.firstName = firstName;
        this.lastName = lastName;
    }

    public String getFirstName() {
        return this.firstName;
    }
```

```
    public String getLastName() {
        return this.lastName;
    }


    public String toString() {
        return "Employee(" + this.firstName + "," + this.
lastName + ")";
    }
}
```

As you can see from this basic example, the code is readable, and we can easily model an employee in the system. When the business requires us to *print a list of all employees* or *add the ability to store an employee's location in their profile*, you can hopefully see how our current Employee class forms the basis to add such functionality.

Now that we have learned what OO code looks like, we can review some of the design patterns that are commonly used and that inspired DDD.

So, what are OOD patterns?

Design patterns were first described in 1977 in a book titled *A Pattern Language: Towns, Buildings, Construction*, by *Christopher Alexander, Oxford University Press*. This book has nothing to do with software engineering, yet it inspired one of the most influential books on OOP design, called *Design Patterns, Elements of Reusable Object-Oriented Software*, by *Erich Gamma, Richard Helm, Ralph Johnson,* and *John Vlissides, Addison-Wesley Professional*. This book was released in 1995 but still features at the top of computer science students' reading lists in 2022. You may have heard of this book by its colloquial name, the **Gang of Four** (or **GoF**), in reference to its four authors.

In the GoF book, 23 design patterns are outlined for what the authors believe lead to scalable, maintainable OO software. Going through each pattern is beyond the scope of this book (the GoF book comprises ~400 pages).

However, if you have read the GoF book, as you proceed to learn more about DDD, it is worth taking a pause and seeing whether you can see where Evans's inspiration came from. The GoF patterns are split into the following sections, which are equally important when considering DDD:

- **Creational patterns** are patterns concerned with creating objects instead of creating objects directly. This gives more flexibility to the program in deciding which object type to create, given the current context.

- **Structural patterns** are concerned with how you compose objects within your program to achieve certain functionality.
- **Behavioral patterns** are concerned with how objects communicate.

Now that we have learned a little about what inspired DDD, let's talk about the book that started it all.

Eric Evans and DDD

Evans's book (sometimes called the *Big Blue Book*) has become a must-read title for all software engineers and architects. Whenever we talk about DDD, this is the book that started it all. In the book, he gave a common language and a set of principles to design systems that have been refined and clarified over the years by members of an ever-growing community.

The *Big Blue Book* has sold over 100,000 copies and consistently remains in the top 10 computing books on Amazon. Martin Fowler, a famous thought leader in the software engineering space, describes the book as "*an essential read for serious software engineers*" (in his *martinFowler.com* blog, *2020*: https://martinfowler.com/bliki/DomainDrivenDesign.html).

However, the book is not without flaws. It has received criticism for being hard to read. In his review, Matt Carroll states: "*The book is written in a dialect approaching that of academia. Big words, long sentences, and introduction to concepts that are so abstract that they would be unintelligible without the accompanying examples. In fact, some parts continue to be unintelligible even with the examples*" (in his *Medium* blog, *2016*: https://mattcarroll.medium.com/book-review-domain-driven-design-42c96a75a72).

Regardless of the criticism, the book is still as relevant and celebrated as it was years ago when it was published. One reason is that the book outlined three pillars that can be used independently or together to improve complex software projects. In the next section, we will review these pillars.

Three pillars of DDD

In this book, Evans introduced three main concepts (sometimes called pillars) of DDD. These are **ubiquitous language**, **strategic design**, and **tactical design**. We have summarized them in this section, but we go into each in more depth later in this book.

Ubiquitous language

Ubiquitous language is the term we use to describe the process of building a common language we can use when talking about our domain. This language should be spoken by everyone in the team—developers and business folk alike. It unites the team by ensuring there is no ambiguity in communication.

As with *real* languages, the ubiquitous language should evolve as your team's understanding of the domain increases. It should never be imposed by domain experts, for it is not a business language. We will discuss how to develop a ubiquitous language in *Chapter 2*.

Strategic design

Strategic design is a phase of the DDD process in which we map out the business domain and define bounded contexts.

The goal of strategic design is to ensure that you architect your system in a way focused on business outcomes. We do this by first mapping out a **domain model**, which is an abstract representation of the problem space. If you were working on a shipping system, your domain model might look like this:

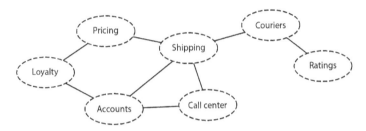

Figure 1.1 – A domain model diagram representing a shipping domain

Notice how shipping is at the center of the diagram? This is part of the core domain, and all the surrounding points are there to support shipping.

There is more work to be done here to create bounded contexts, but even at this very early stage of the DDD process, you can start to think about how your system might look.

We will talk about bounded contexts in much more detail in *Chapter 2*.

Tactical design

Tactical design is where we begin to get into the specifics of how our system will look. In the tactical design phase, we begin talking about **entities**, **aggregates**, and **value objects**, which also happens to be the title of *Chapter 3* of this book. We will use these patterns to help us define software boundaries.

Adoption of DDD

DDD has remained popular since its inception, as depicted in the following screenshot, which shows a trend line in a *Google Trends* graph.

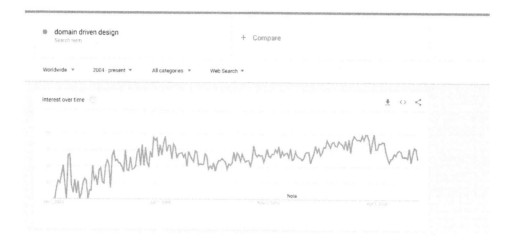

Figure 1.2 – Google Trends graph of searches for DDD

Indeed, it is just as valuable to learn DDD (maybe more so) now as in 2004 (as far back as *Google Trends* goes).

Although Evans laid the foundation for DDD, it has remained relevant for nearly 2 decades because, in Evans's own words, *"smart and innovative people have shaken things up repeatedly."* These people have taken the fundamentals outlined in a DDD and created new concepts, which have enabled DDD to remain relevant, even though the way we write software has changed quite dramatically.

Some of the books highlighted by Evans are listed here:

- Greg Young and his work on **Command Query Responsibility Segregation (CQRS)**: CQRS is a pattern that emerged to capture all application changes as a sequence of events. It allows the segregation of read and write events from the database and can help maximize application performance, scalability, and security. This is particularly popular in large enterprise software.

- *Domain-Driven Design Quickly*: This book was released in 2006 and was (and still is) free; you can read it here: https://www.infoq.com/minibooks/domain-driven-design-quickly/. Evans likes this book as its simple and succinct nature made DDD accessible to everyone.

- Vaughn Vernon and his book *Implementing Domain-Driven Design*: Evans described Vernon's book as *"the most ambitious book since my own."* The community has affectionately called this book the *Big Red Book*. This book refreshed a lot of the ideas that Evans outlined originally and focused more on *how* you can implement DDD.

Big companies such as Microsoft, Amazon, and IBM use DDD internally and guide how you can use it too. It is, therefore, still a great time investment to learn about DDD today.

Is DDD always applicable though? Just because big companies use it, it does not necessarily mean it is a good fit for your side project. In the next section, we explore this in more detail.

When should you use DDD?

DDD works best when applied to large, complex systems. A surprising number of the systems Software engineers write today are basic **CRUD** (short for **create, read, update**, and **delete**) applications. Applying DD development to such applications would be overkill and likely make delivery slower and more complicated.

The *Big Red Book* provides a helpful **DDD scorecard**. Here is a simplified version of the scorecard:

Is your project . . .	Points	Additional thoughts
Mostly doing simple create, reads, updates, and deletes from the database?	0	Sometimes, evaluating *simple* can be tricky. If you have lots of business logic between the input and the output, your application might not fit into this category. If all you are doing is validating the input and then passing it through to the database layer, you are in this category.
Does your application have fewer than 30 user stories/business flows?	1	User stories often take this format—as a user, I want an X so that I can Y. Does your system have 30 of these flows? Is it likely to have much more in the future, or are changes mostly minor updates at this point? If it's fewer than 30, don't give your system the point here.
Does your application have 40+ user/stories/business flows?	2	We're starting to enter the territory where we might want to consider DDD. Vaughn correctly highlights that we often do not identify complexity early enough and must pay for that decision later. Consider this your early warning that you are likely building a complex system.
Is the application likely to grow in complexity?	3	Some applications start simple, but there is a clear path to complexity. For example, if you were bootstrapping a startup, you might have something simple for the first few months. But as you attract funding, you know you will have to step up the complexity of the problem you're solving.

The application will be around for a long time, and the changes you predict you need to make will not be simple.	4	There are very few systems that don't undergo regular change. Understanding the complexity of the changes necessary is important to deciding whether DDD is right for you. Updating a holiday booking system to understand next year's public holidays versus making a crypto exchange to support a new protocol are different classes of problems—the latter being worthy of the points for this category.
You don't understand the domain because it is new, and as far as you are aware, no one has ever built a system like this before.	5	Modeling and defining a domain is DDD's bread and butter.

Table 1.1 – DDD scorecard

If you score more than 7 points on the table, your application is a great candidate for DDD.

If you have scored less than 7, you may still benefit from some of the principles we will discuss in this book, but it might be that the time investment necessary to implement DDD *properly* is not worth it.

Committing to following the DDD principles is precisely that—a commitment. It cannot come from engineering; it needs to be a decision involving all project stakeholders. It requires time and effort to get the domain, language, and contexts correct and needs strong involvement from the domain experts. It also requires engineers to think one level higher than software and to think about behavior first.

Summary

In this chapter, we have explored the context in which DDD came to exist, its adoption over time, and an overview of some core concepts. We ended the chapter by highlighting a simple score system that you can use as a reference when discussing DDD adoption with your team.

You should now understand the context of how DDD emerged and have an idea of when it might be appropriate to use it.

In the next chapter. we will dig deeper into some of the core concepts of DDD as we discuss ubiquitous language, bounded context, domains, and subdomains.

Further reading

For more information, please refer to the following resources:

- *Design a DDD-oriented microservice* by Microsoft (2022); available at `https://docs.microsoft.com/en-us/dotnet/architecture/microservices/microservice-ddd-cqrs-patterns/ddd-oriented-microservice`

- *Find Your Business Domains to Start Refactoring Monolithic Applications* by **Amazon Web Services (AWS)** (2022); available at `https://aws.amazon.com/blogs/mt/find-your-business-domains-to-start-refactoring-monolithic-applications/`

- *Apply Domain-Driven Design to microservices architecture* by IBM; available at `https://www.ibm.com/garage/method/practices/code/domain-driven-design/`

2

Understanding Domains, Ubiquitous Language, and Bounded Contexts

In this chapter, we will introduce some of the core concepts of **domain-driven design** (**DDD**). For those who have never worked with DDD before, it should cover enough of the details so that you understand the fundamental concepts. For those with more experience, it should serve as a refresher. I hope that after you have completed this book, you will also be able to use this chapter as a reference when applying DDD in the real world.

I have used real-life scenarios wherever possible to make things as clear as possible. This starts with the *Setting the scene* section, so be sure to read that even if you're skimming!

By the end of the chapter, you should be able to answer the following questions:

- What is a domain?

- What is a sub-domain?

- What does ubiquitous language mean?

- What is a bounded context?

Technical requirements

In this chapter, we will write a small amount of Golang code. To be able to run it, you will need the following:

- **Golang installation**: You can find instructions to install it here: `https://go.dev/doc/install`. The code in this chapter was written with Go 1.19.3 installed, so anything later than this should be fine.

- **A text editor or IDE:** Some popular options are VS Code (`https://code.visualstudio.com/download`) and GoLand (`https://www.jetbrains.com/help/go/installation-guide.html`).

- **GitHub repository:** `https://github.com/PacktPublishing/Domain-Driven-Design-with-GoLang/tree/main/chapter2`.

Setting the scene

You have recently been promoted to be the team lead for a brand-new engineering team in your company, the *payments and subscriptions* team. As this is a new area for you, you diligently organize time with experts in the department to discuss the basics of the **domain** and how it works. Here is their response:

"When a *lead* uses our app for the first time, they must pick one of three *subscription plans*. These are *basic*, *premium*, and *exclusive*. Depending on which they pick determines which *features* they get access to within the app. This may change over time. Once a *subscription plan* has been created, we consider that the *lead* has converted to a *customer*, and we call them a *customer* until they *churn*. At this point, we call them a *lead* again. After 6 months, we call them a *lost lead* and we might target them with a *re-engagement campaign*, which could include a *discount code*. Once a *plan* is created, we set up a *recurring payment* to *capture funds* from the *customer* by *direct debit*."

Excitedly, you run off and define the following interfaces as a starting point for the new application your team will be building:

```go
package chapter2

import (
    "context"
)

type UserType = int
type SubscriptionType = int

const (
    unknownUserType UserType = iota
    lead
    customer
    churned
    lostLead
)
```

```go
const (
    unknownSubscriptionType SubscriptionType = iota
    basic
    premium
    exclusive
)

type UserAddRequest struct {
    UserType       UserType
    Email          string
    SubType        SubscriptionType
    PaymentDetails PaymentDetails
}

type UserModifyRequest struct {
    ID             string
    UserType       UserType
    Email          string
    SubType        SubscriptionType
    PaymentDetails PaymentDetails
}

type User struct {
    ID             string
    PaymentDetails PaymentDetails
}

type PaymentDetails struct {
    stripeTokenID string
}

type UserManager interface {
    AddUser(ctx context.Context, request UserAddRequest) (User,
error)
    ModifyUser(ctx context.Context, request UserModifyRequest)
(User, error)
}
```

We'll revisit this as we learn more about DDD.

Domains and sub-domains

In the *Setting the scene* section, we outlined that we are going to be building a payments and subscriptions system. These are our domains. According to Eric Evans, domains are *"a sphere of knowledge, influence, or activity."* (*Domain-Driven Design*, Addison-Wesley Professional).

The domain is the central entity in DDD; it is what we will model our entire language and system around. Another way to think of it is the world of business. Every time you read the phrase *domain-driven design*, you could read it as *business problem-driven design*.

Deciding on domains is a challenging problem and not always as obvious as in our example. In our example, we have two distinct domains—**payments** and **subscriptions**. Some teams may choose to treat these both as a single domain, which would be fine, too; DDD is not a science.

Bigger companies will often organize their teams around domains. In a mature organization, this will be a discussion that includes stakeholders from all departments to land on an organizational structure that makes sense. As new domains are discovered and teams grow, teams may split into new domain-based teams.

Domains and **sub-domains** can be used almost interchangeably. We tend to use a sub-domain to signal that the domain we are talking about is a child of a higher-level domain. In our example, we know that our payment and subscription domains are sub-domains of a much larger business domain. Therefore, we may refer to them as **sub-domains**, depending on the context of our conversation.

Ubiquitous language

Ubiquitous language is the overlap of the language that domain experts and technical experts use. The following Venn diagram highlights this:

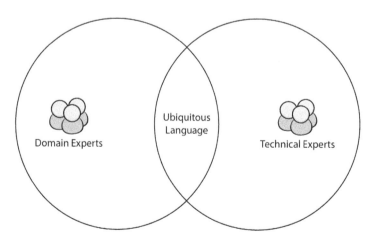

Figure 2.1 – Ubiquitous language

In the *Setting the scene* section, we highlighted interesting words that the experts used in your conversation. That language has a specific meaning in your team that might not hold for other companies or teams. For example, what is referred to as a *customer* in your team might mean something slightly different to the marketing team.

The highlighted words are your team's ubiquitous language. It is a shared language, unique and specific to your team. Whenever your team talks about a *customer* or a *lost lead*, there should be no confusion about what this means. It is often helpful to keep a glossary of terms in your team's wiki or documentation that is reviewed regularly. Although domain experts are fundamental to definitions, engineers must challenge them and think about edge cases to ensure the definitions are robust.

This language should be used when discussing requirements and system design and should even be used in the source code itself. Plus, it should evolve; therefore, you should spend time evaluating and updating it regularly (perhaps during sprint planning if you're an agile team).

This sounds like a lot of effort, so let's discuss the benefits of using it.

Benefits of ubiquitous language

One of the major reasons IT projects fail is because a requirement *got lost in translation*. For example, the business folks asked their team to support multiple accounts per customer. However, due to historical decisions and assumptions made about the business, their system doesn't have a customer entity. There were strong assumptions made all over the system that there would only ever be one user per account. What could have potentially been a trivial change is now a hugely risky project that could span multiple quarters. Furthermore, notice the use of the term *user* and not the term *customer* in the description. This seems a minor distinction, but the fact the engineers were not thinking in terms of the business and using ubiquitous language is likely a reason this important invariant was missed.

We mentioned that our ubiquitous language should be used in the source code itself. Let's take another look at some of the code we wrote in the *Setting the scene* section:

```
type UserType = int
type subscriptionType = int

const (
    unknownUserType UserType = iota
    lead
    customer
    churned
    lostLead
)
```

```
const (
    unknownSubscriptionType subscriptionType = iota
    basic
    premium
    exclusive
)
```

We have done a good job here of using ubiquitous language in our source code. Whenever the domain experts talk about a *subscription*, we do not need to do any mental gymnastics to find a system representation of it.

We also created a `userType`, but the discussion we had with the domain experts did not mention the term *user* at all. This would be a good opportunity to discuss this specific term and add it to your team's ubiquitous language glossary to ensure when we use the term *user*, we are all talking about the same thing.

Some further code we wrote was this:

```
type UserAddRequest struct {
    userType       UserType
    email          string
    subType        subscriptionType
    paymentDetails PaymentDetails
}

type UserModifyRequest struct {
    id             string
    userType       UserType
    email          string
    subType        subscriptionType
    paymentDetails PaymentDetails
}

type User struct {
    id string
}

type PaymentDetails struct {
    stripeTokenID string
```

```
}

type UserManager interface {
    AddUser(ctx context.Context, request UserAddRequest) (User,
error)
    ModifyUser(ctx context.Context, request UserModifyRequest)
(User, error)
}
```

At first sight, the rest of the code looks reasonable; I am sure you have seen code such as this before.

Let's assume we worked with the domain experts and agreed on a definition for the term *user* as *a way to represent any persons using our app (or who have used our app) no matter their status*. The possible states are *lead*, *lost lead*, *customer*, and *churned*, but we may discover more in the future. Given this definition, the `AddUser` function now doesn't seem like such a good idea. Our domain doesn't have the concept of adding users, and using this phrase with domain experts is likely to confuse them. We are going to end up with a mapping between a system representation of the domain and a real-world representation. We are not benefiting from the time we have invested to come up with a robust ubiquitous language.

If we go back to the brief, we see that someone new to the app is called a *lead*, and once they select a subscription, they convert into a *customer*. Given this, we can make some amendments to our code, as follows:

```
type LeadRequest struct {
    email string
}

type Lead struct {
    id string
}

type LeadCreator interface {
    CreateLead(ctx context.Context, request LeadRequest) (Lead,
error)
}

type Customer struct {
    leadID string
    userID string
```

```go
}

func (c *Customer) UserID() string {
    return c.userID
}

func (c *Customer) SetUserID(userID string) {
    c.userID = userID
}

type LeadConvertor interface {
    Convert(ctx context.Context, subSelection SubscriptionType)
(Customer, error)
}

func (l Lead) Convert(ctx context.Context, subSelection
SubscriptionType) (Customer, error) {
    //TODO implement me
    panic("implement me")
}
```

This code is much more reasonable and reflects the real world much better. Now, when we discuss our system with our experts, we can talk in terms of leads, converting leads, customers, and subscriptions—all ubiquitous language to our domain.

How do you ensure you capture all ubiquitous language?

There are no shortcuts to building a robust, ubiquitous language; it takes time. Spending lots of time with domain experts is the best way to ensure you capture all important languages. One way to do this is to ask whether you can join their meetings and perhaps offer to take the minutes. During the meeting, you should write down any terms you did not understand and afterward follow up to get a definition. Ensure you add this to the glossary of terms and share this with the rest of your colleagues.

A warning on the application of ubiquitous language

It can be tempting to try to apply a ubiquitous language across multiple projects, teams, and even across an entire company. However, if you do this, you are setting yourself up for failure. Evans advises that ubiquitous language should only apply to a single **bounded context** (we talk about the bounded context in the next section, but for now, you can think of bounded context as our project team and the system we proposed in the *Setting the scene* section). The reason for this is that ubiquitous language works best when it is rigorous. If you try to make a specific word (especially, loaded terms such as *customer* or *user*) apply to all different areas of your business, the term will lose that rigor, and confusion will reign.

Bounded contexts

We have the beginnings of an outline for our subscription system. We have even described some ubiquitous language to describe the system. What if someone from a different area of a business came to discuss *customers* with us? The first thing we should do is define what a customer means to them as it may mean something different within their bounded context.

Bounded contexts are all about dividing large models into smaller, easier-to-understand chunks and being explicit about how they relate to each other.

Another way to think of them is a boundary—when we define a term in one context, it does not need to mean the same in another (although there are likely similarities). For example, if we were to draw a diagram for our subscription system, it might look like this:

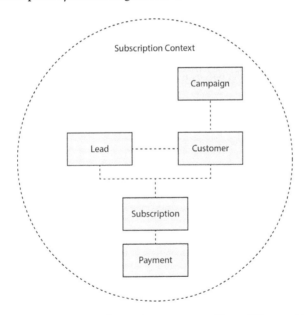

Figure 2.2 – A domain map of our subscription context and how different objects are related

But after speaking to marketing and understanding their context just a little bit, we might define the following relationships:

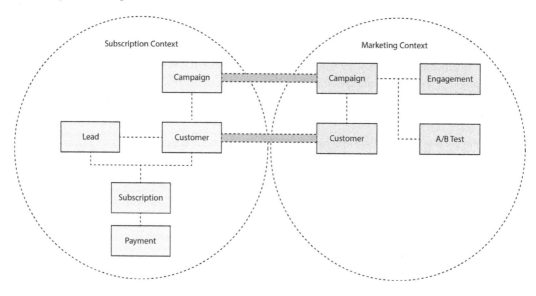

Figure 2.3 – Mapping between marketing and subscription contexts

The lines between campaign and customer in the different bounded contexts represent that, although the same term is used, the model is different, and we can expect to do some mapping between them. This is discussed in detail in the following paragraphs.

We have clarified here that both contexts care about *campaigns* and *customers*, but how we model it and talk about it in each context does not need to be the same. This is a simple example, but as systems evolve and gain complexity, defining boundaries makes more and more sense.

Since several bounded contexts often must communicate as shown in *Figure 2.3*, we often apply patterns to ensure our models can maintain integrity. The three main patterns are as follows:

- Open Host Service
- Published language
- Anti-corruption layer

Let's explore these patterns in more detail.

Open Host Service

An **Open Host Service** is a means of giving other systems (or sub-systems) access to ours. Evans leaves it purposefully ambiguous as its implementation depends on your team's skill sets and other constraints (for example, if you are working with legacy applications, some of the modern **Remote Procedure Call (RPC)** approaches discussed here might not be viable to you). Typically, an Open Host Service is an RPC. Some choices for RPCs might be to build a RESTful API, implement gRPC, or perhaps even an XML API!

Here is a visual example of what an Open Host Service might look like:

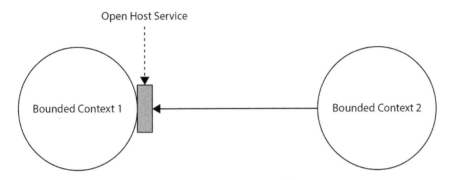

Figure 2.4 – An Open Host Service

In this diagram, the rectangle represents an *exposed* piece of our bounded context.

Let's apply what we have learned about Open Host Service to our example.

For our payments and subscription example, we might expose an endpoint to allow the marketing team to get various kinds of information about a user within our context, such as this:

```
package chapter2

import (
    "context"
    "encoding/json"
    "net/http"

    "github.com/gorilla/mux"
)

type UserHandler interface {
    IsUserSubscriptionActive(ctx context.Context, userID
string) bool
}
```

```
type UserActiveResponse struct {
    IsActive bool
}


func router(u UserHandler) {
    m := mux.NewRouter()
    m.HandleFunc("/user/{userID}/subscription/active",
func(writer http.ResponseWriter, request *http.Request) {
        // check auth, etc

        uID := mux.Vars(request)["userID"]
        if uID == "" {
            writer.WriteHeader(http.StatusBadRequest)
            return
        }
        isActive := u.IsUserSubscriptionActive(request.
Context(), uID)

        b, err := json.Marshal(UserActiveResponse{IsActive:
isActive})
        if err != nil {
            writer.WriteHeader(http.StatusInternalServerError)
            return
        }
        _, _ = writer.Write(b)
    }).Methods(http.MethodGet)
}
```

The preceding code block exposes a simple endpoint over HTTP available at /user/{userID}/ subscription/active that could be used by another team to check whether a user has an active subscription or not.

Published language

A ubiquitous language is our team's internal formally defined language; a published language is the opposite. If our team is going to expose some of our systems to other teams via an **Open Host Service**, we need to ensure the definition of what we expose to other teams in **different bounded contexts** is clear.

If we were to extend our HTTP server mentioned earlier to have a `GET /{id}/user` endpoint, we would need to publish language to help other teams understand the output schema. Two popular ways to present published language are via **OpenAPI** or **gRPC**.

OpenAPI

We can use OpenAPI to define the schema. This is a popular approach as you can also generate client and server code to speed up development for your team and for consumer teams too. You can use a tool called **Swagger** for this. The code might look something like this:

```
swagger: "2.0"
info:
  description: "Public documentation for payment & subscription
System"
  version: "1.0.0"
  title: "Payment & Subscription API"
  contact:
    email: "ourteam@subs.com"
host: "api.payments.com"
schemes:
  - "https"
paths:
  /users:
    get:
      summary: "Return details about users"
      operationId: "getUsers"
      produces:
        - "application/json"
      responses:
        "200":
          description: "successful operation"
          schema:
            $ref: "#/definitions/User"
        "400":
          description: "bad request"
        "404":
          description: "users not found"
  definitions:
```

```
User:
  type: "object"
  properties:
    id:
      type: "integer"
      format: "int64"
    username:
      type: "string"
    subscriptionStatus:
      type: "boolean"
    subscriptionType:
      type: "string"
    email:
      type: "string"
ApiResponse:
  type: "object"
  properties:
    code:
      type: "integer"
      format: "int32"
    type:
      type: "string"
    message:
      type: "string"
```

This code generates the following easy-to-digest UI, which we can share with other teams as our published language:

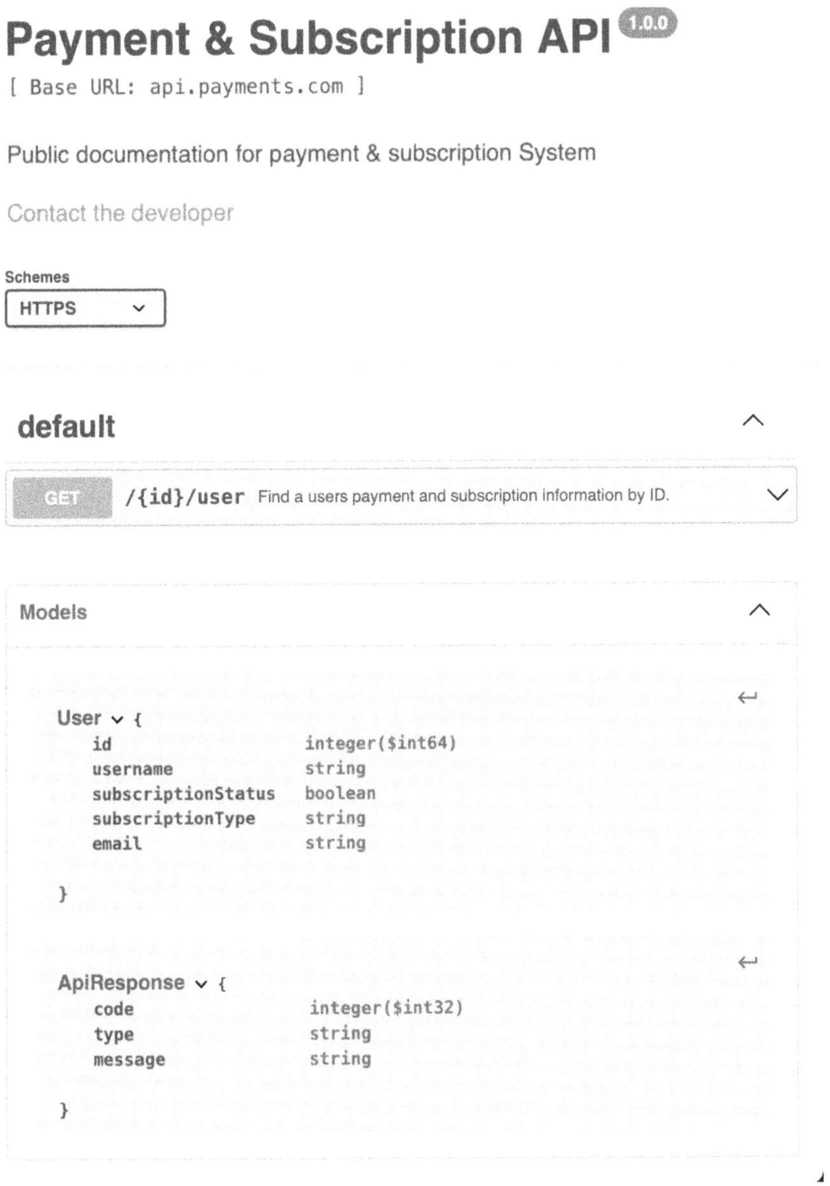

Payment & Subscription API 1.0.0

[Base URL: api.payments.com]

Public documentation for payment & subscription System

Contact the developer

Schemes

```
HTTPS     ∨
```

default   ∧

```
GET    /{id}/user   Find a users payment and subscription information by ID.    ∨
```

Models   ∧

```
                                                                    ↵
    User ∨ {
        id                  integer($int64)
        username            string
        subscriptionStatus  boolean
        subscriptionType    string
        email               string

    }


                                                                    ↵
    ApiResponse ∨ {
        code                integer($int32)
        type                string
        message             string

    }
```

Figure 2.5 – The generated API documentation for the OpenAPI specification

If you want to play around and generate your own OpenAPI code from a specification, you can use the Swagger Editor (`https://editor.swagger.io`) in your browser.

As well as generating documentation, Swagger also enables you to generate client and server code in a variety of different languages and frameworks:

ada-server	jaxrs-cxf-cdi	python-flask
aspnetcore	jaxrs-resteasy	rails5
erlang-server	jaxrs-resteasy-eap	restbed
finch	jaxrs-spec	rust-server
go-server	kotlin-server	scala-lagom-server
haskell	lumen	scalatra
inflector	msf4j	sinatra
java-pkmst	nancyfx	slim
java-play-framework	nodejs-server	spring
java-vertx	php-silex	undertow
jaxrs	php-symfony	ze-ph
jaxrs-cxf	pistache-server	

Figure 2.6 – Languages supported by Swagger

For Go specifically, I have had a lot of success using `oapi-codegen` (`https://github.com/deepmap/oapi-codegen`). `oapi-codegen` supports generating Go clients and servers from OpenAPI specifications such as the one we created previously. It contains plenty of configuration options and supports multiple server libraries, such as `gorilla` and `chi`. Let's see how we can use it and step through the generated code. You can find all the code and configuration in the GitHub repository for this book here: `https://github.com/PacktPublishing/Domain-Driven-Design-with-GoLang/tree/main/chapter2/oapi`.

Firstly, we have created a configuration file. This tells the `open-api` generator which go package we would like our generated code to be in and which file to store the generated code in. It looks like this:

```
package: oapi
output: ./openapi.gen.go
generate:
  models: true
```

We now need to install the `open-api` generator. We can do this with the following command:

```
go install github.com/deepmap/oapi-codegen/cmd/oapi-codegen@
latest
```

After this is installed, we simply need to run the following command from within the `chapter2/oapi` folder:

```
oapi-codegen --config=config.yml  ./oapi.yaml
```

If all goes well, you should see an `openapi.gen.go` file is created:

Figure 2.7 – openapi.gen.go file

If you see some errors when you open the file, it's likely because we don't have all the necessary Go modules synced to our project. If you run the following, the errors should go away:

```
go mod tidy && go mod vendor
```

You now have an interface for a server that you can implement. Every time you update your API documentation, you can rerun this command to generate a new server definition.

Generating a Go client is especially easy. All we need to do is add `client: true` to our config file. So, `config.yml` now looks like this:

```
package: oapi
output: ./openapi.gen.go
generate:
  models: true
  client: true
```

Our generated code now has a new `Client` definition:

```
// The interface specification for the client above.
type ClientInterface interface {
    // GetUsers request
    GetUsers(ctx context.Context, reqEditors ...RequestEditorFn)
(*http.Response, error)
}
```

Again, if we updated our OpenAPI specification and wanted to update the client, all we would need to do is run the preceding command again. You could set up a job as part of your **continuous integration** (**CI**) pipeline that generates a new client package every time a specification change is made, allowing consumer teams to get the latest version whenever they need it.

As an exercise, see whether you can implement the OpenAPI server and call it with the generated Go client. You may find the examples from `oapi-gen` useful—you can find them here: `https://github.com/deepmap/oapi-codegen/tree/master/examples`.

OpenAPI is a great option for your published language if you and your team are already familiar with REST APIs. OpenAPI is documentation-first, which means your external-facing documentation is always kept up to date, which is a huge advantage. The code generation means you can support many different use cases with no extra effort.

The downside to OpenAPI is that there are more performant alternatives out there. Furthermore, OpenAPI does not give any protection for breaking changes natively. For example, if you removed a field from your documentation, but another team depended on it, you would likely break their workflow.

An alternative, modern approach that solves some of these issues and adds some more features is **gRPC**.

gRPC

gRPC was created at Google to handle remote communication at scale. It supports load balancing, tracing, health checks, bi-directional streaming, and authentication. Usually, these are features you needed to provision other software services or even hardware for in the past.

Furthermore, gRPC uses **binary serialization** to compress the payload it sends, making it very efficient and fast. In gRPC, a client application can call a method on a remote server as if it were local code. gRPC supports a variety of different languages and frameworks, such as OpenAPI.

Here is a visual example of how a gRPC client and server may interact:

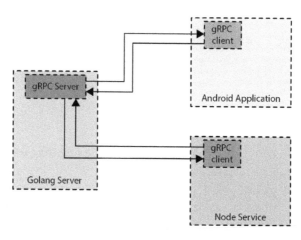

Figure 2.8 – gRPC clients in Node and Kotlin connecting to a gRPC server written in Golang

To call a method on a remote server, firstly, we must define our message **protobuf**. Protobufs are typically defined in a `.proto` file, and they are language-agnostic. A basic (incomplete) example might look like this:

```
message User {
    int64 id = 1;
    string username = 2;
    string email = 3;
}
```

From here, we need to define our service. This is effectively our request and response objects:

```
// The User service definition.
service UserService {
  // Create a User
  rpc CreateUser (CreateUserRequest) returns
(CreateUserResponse) {}
}


// The request message contains all the things we need to
create a user.
message CreateUserRequest {
  User user = 1;
}


// The response message contains whether we were successful or
not
message CreateUserResponse {
  bool success = 1;
}
```

From here, we can generate client and server code, as described earlier.

At the time of writing, gRPC supports the following natively:

- C#
- C++
- Dart
- Golang

- Java

- Kotlin

- Node

- Objective-C

- PHP

- Python

- Ruby

. . . but there are community-built generators for other languages.

gRPC is more complicated to start with than OpenAPI, mostly because developers have generally had more experience with REST-based APIs. Furthermore, some of the tools needed to generate code can be quite complicated to install and get working. Let's see what that looks like in Go.

gRPC for Go using buf

We are going to use buf (https://buf.build) to generate our Go client and server as I have found it by far the most accessible way to interact with protobuf.

First, let's install some of the underlying protobuf tools we will need with the following commands:

```
go install google.golang.org/protobuf/cmd/protoc-gen-go@latest
go install google.golang.org/grpc/cmd/protoc-gen-go-grpc@latest
```

You also need to update your path with the following command:

```
export PATH="$PATH:$(go env GOPATH)/bin"
```

Next, let's make a file called buf.gen.yml. It looks like this:

```
version: v1
plugins:
  - name: go
    out: gen/proto/go
    opt: paths=source_relative
  - name: go-grpc
    out: gen/proto/go
    opt:
      - paths=source_relative
      - require_unimplemented_servers=false
```

You can also find the code for this here: `https://github.com/PacktPublishing/Domain-Driven-Design-with-GoLang/tree/main/chapter2/grpc`. The preceding code simply says we want to generate Go from our protobuf definition. You can add C, Java, and other languages here too.

Let's now install `buf`:

```
brew install bufbuild/buf/buf
```

To verify everything is running correctly, if you run `buf lint` from `chapter2/grpc`, you should see the following output:

```
user.proto:1:1:Files must have a package defined.
```

Let's fix this by adding a package to the top of the file:

```
syntax = "proto3";
package user.v1;



message User {
    int64 id = 1;
    string username = 2;
    string email = 3;
}


// The User service definition.
service UserService {
    // Create a User
    rpc CreateUser (CreateUserRequest) returns
(CreateUserResponse) {}
}


// The request message contains all the things we need to
create a user.
message CreateUserRequest {
    User user = 1;
}
```

```
// The response message contains whether we were successful or
not
message CreateUserResponse {
  bool success = 1;
}
```

If you rerun the `buf lint` command, you should now see no output.

Now, we can run the following command to generate our gRPC client and server:

buf generate

We now experience what will be our final error:

```
protoc-gen-go: unable to determine Go import path for "user/v1/
user.proto"

Please specify either:
        • a "go_package" option in the .proto source file, or
        • a "M" argument on the command line.

See https://developers.google.com/protocol-buffers/docs/
reference/go-generated#package for more information.

Failure: plugin go: exit status 1
```

The `protobuf` tooling comes with lots of opinions and support to ensure best practices. Let's add a package name for our `protobuf` file, making the final file look like this:

```
syntax = "proto3";
package user.v1;
option go_package = "example.com/testing/protos/user";


message User {
  int64 id = 1;
  string username = 2;
  string email = 3;
}
```

```
// The User service definition.
service UserService {
  // Create a User
  rpc CreateUser (CreateUserRequest) returns
(CreateUserResponse) {}
}


// The request message contains all the things we need to
create a user.
message CreateUserRequest {
  User user = 1;
}


// The response message contains whether we were successful or
not
message CreateUserResponse {
  bool success = 1;
}
```

If we run buf generate one final time, we will see that a gen folder has been created for us with importable Go code:

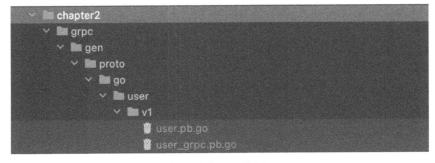

Figure 2.9 – gen folder

As an exercise, see if you can implement the gRPC client and server. The buf docs give guidance on how you might do that here: https://docs.buf.build/tour/implement-grpc-endpoints.

Which should you choose?

Either! You will have great results with either approach. Due to gRPC's speed and extra features, it is becoming more popular. However, OpenAPI can be easier to retrofit to already existing APIs and is easier to understand.

Anti-corruption layer

Sometimes called an **adapter layer**, an **anti-corruption layer** can be used to translate models from different systems. It is a complementary pattern that works well with the Open Host Service. For example, the marketing team's published language may define a campaign as follows:

```
{
    "id":"4cdd4ba9-7c04-4a3d-ac52-71f37ba75d7f",
    "metadata":{
        "name":"some campaign",
        "category":"growth",
        "endDate":"2023-04-12"
    }
}
```

However, our internal model for a campaign might look like this:

```
type Campaign struct {
    id       string
    title    string
    goal     string
    endDate time.Time
}
```

As you can see, we care about most of the same information, but we name it differently or have a slightly different format. We have two options here:

- We can swap our campaign model to be exactly the same as the marketing model. This would go against the principles of DDD and mean we are strongly coupling the domain model to something outside of our control.

- We can write an anti-corruption layer.

An anti-corruption later would look like this:

```
package chapter2

import (
    "errors"
    "time"
)
```

```go
type Campaign struct {
    ID      string
    Title   string
    Goal    string
    EndDate time.Time
}

type MarketingCampaignModel struct {
    Id       string `json:"id"`
    Metadata struct {
        Name     string `json:"name"`
        Category string `json:"category"`
        EndDate  string `json:"endDate"`
    } `json:"metadata"`
}

func (m *MarketingCampaignModel) ToCampaign() (*Campaign,
error) {
    if m.Id == "" {
        return nil, errors.New("campaign ID cannot be empty")
    }
    formattedDate, err := time.Parse("2006-01-02", m.Metadata.
EndDate)
    if err != nil {
        return nil, errors.New("endDate was not in a parsable
format")
    }

    return &Campaign{
        ID:      m.Id,
        Title:   m.Metadata.Name,
        Goal:    m.Metadata.Category,
        EndDate: formattedDate,
    }, nil
}
```

In this short snippet, we translated a `MarketingCampaignModel` into a `Campaign` in our domain. We included some checks to ensure the format of the data we receive is acceptable and won't corrupt our data model. It's worth noting that in more complex systems, anti-corruption layers could be entire services. This can be useful when you intend to migrate from an old system to a new system in multiple stages. However, it adds another point of latency and failure. The following diagram provides an example of an anti-corruption layer:

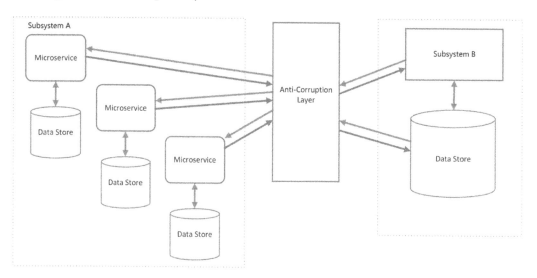

Figure 2.10 – Anti-corruption layer in a distributed system

Of all the DDD patterns, the anti-corruption pattern is the one I use most when working on systems that do not use DDD. It's simple but very effective for ensuring we keep systems decoupled.

Summary

In this chapter, we have learned about domains, sub-domains, ubiquitous language, and bounded contexts. These are all core components of DDD.

We explored some domain-driven Go code for the first time and saw how even minor changes could improve the readability of our code and make it align more with the domain we are developing software for.

We also learned about some new patterns—Open Host Service, published language, and anti-corruption layers. Finally, we explored some tools (OpenAPI and gRPC) we can use to make publishing language easier.

In the next chapter, *Aggregates, Entities, and Value Objects*, we will explore more DDD terminology and learn how these concepts can help make our domain-driven code more robust and scalable.

Further reading

- OpenAPI: `https://github.com/OAI/OpenAPI-Specification`
- Swagger: `https://swagger.io`
- gRPC: `https://grpc.io`

3

Entities, Value Objects, and Aggregates

In the previous chapter, we learned about some of the core concepts of domain-driven design. In this chapter, we will build upon that foundational knowledge to learn more patterns and concepts, which will help you on your journey to mastering DDD. We will start by looking at entities and value objects. This is where we will write most of the business logic for our domain-driven application.

We will finish by looking at aggregates, which are useful when we need to cluster domain objects together and treat them as a single item.

In this chapter, we will cover the following topics:

- What is an entity, and how should I use it?
- What are some common pitfalls when designing entities, and how can I avoid them?
- What is a value object, and how should I use it?
- What is the aggregate pattern, and how should I use it?
- How do I discover aggregates?

By the end of this chapter, you will be able to identify some common pitfalls while designing entities and how we can avoid them. You will also be able to tell what value objects and aggregate patterns are and to use them.

Let's start by looking at entities.

Technical requirements

In this chapter, we will write a small amount of Golang code. To be able to run it, you will need the following:

- **Golang installation:** You can find instructions on how to install it here: `https://go.dev/doc/install`. The code in this chapter was written with Go 1.19.3 installed, so anything later than this should be fine.

- **A text editor or IDE:** Some popular options are VSCode (`https://code.visualstudio.com/download`) and Goland (`https://www.jetbrains.com/help/go/installation-guide.html`).

- **GitHub repository:** `https://github.com/PacktPublishing/Domain-Driven-Design-with-GoLang/tree/main/chapter3`.

Working with entities

In domain-driven design, entities are defined by their identity. Their attributes do not define them, and it is expected that although their attributes may change over time, their identity will not. While the entity may change so much that it is indistinguishable from where it started, it retains the same identity, and we treat it as the same object. Let's look at an example. On ebay.com, you can sign up as a user. If you choose to sell something, you become a seller. You can also choose to bid on items. A naïve model of this might look as follows:

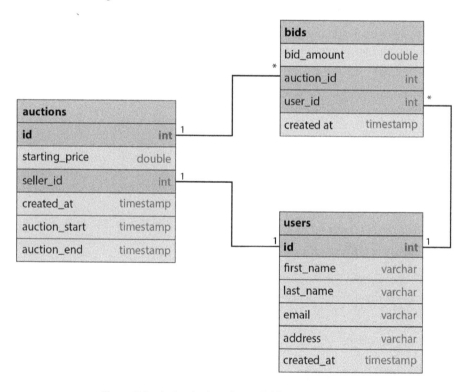

Figure 3.1 – A simple domain model for an auction site

Some actions that could take place in our system are as follows:

- A user updates their address
- A user updates their email address
- An auction end time is updated

These actions do not change the *identity* of our entity. We are still referencing the same ID, but some attributes may have changed.

An implementation of the auction entity might look as follows:

```
package chapter3

import (
    "time"

    "github.com/Rhymond/go-money"
)

// Auction is an entity to represent our auction construct.
type Auction struct {
    ID int
    // We use a specific money library as floats are not good
ways to represent money.
    startingPrice money.Money
    sellerID      int
    createdAt     time.Time
    auctionStart  time.Time
    auctionEnd    time.Time
}
```

As an exercise, see if you can write entities for bids and users.

In the preceding code sample, we have an int called ID – this is our entity ID. Entity IDs do not necessarily have to be generated by the system. They may form part of the entity's attributes. For example, in most countries, people are issued a unique tax identification number that never changes. Therefore, it might be a good unique identifier for you to use if it's relevant to your domain (for example, if you are building a HR system).

One interesting case is a user's email address. At a glance, email addresses might seem like good entity identifiers as we will require them to be unique. However, in most systems, users can change the email address they will receive notifications on. Therefore, email addresses would be much better suited to be an attribute of the entity.

Generating good identifiers

Generating good unique identifiers for our entities is surprisingly hard. In the previous example, we used an `int` for our ID. For some good use cases, this will be fine as it is simple. However, in a system of substantial scale, we will quickly run into an issue.

Let's say we write the following Go code:

```
fmt.Println(math.MaxInt)
```

We will get the following output:

```
9223372036854775807
```

However, let's try and add 1 to this:

```
fmt.Println(math.MaxInt + 1)
```

We will get the following error:

```
cannot use math.MaxInt + 1 (untyped int constant
9223372036854775808) as int value in argument to fmt.Println
(overflows)
```

We just ran out of integers! If we had used this as an identifier, we would now be experiencing a customer-facing production issue and would need to scramble to rearchitect our system under pressure effectively.

It is essential to try and future-proof your system as much as possible, especially when it comes to things such as entity identifiers. If you struggle to develop a good strategy for generating IDs, using **universally unique identifiers** (**UUIDs**) is a good place to start. UUIDs are 128-bit labels, which, when generated according to the specification, are effectively unique.

While UUIDs are not a part of the Go standard library, Google provides an excellent library for them. The following is an example of how to use UUIDs in Go:

```
package chapter3


import "github.com/google/uuid"
```

```
type SomeEntity struct {
    id uuid.UUID
}

func NewSomeEntity() *SomeEntity {
    id := uuid.New()
    return &SomeEntity{id: id}
}
```

If you are using a persistent store such as PostgreSQL, you can lean on it to create a UUID for you.

A warning when defining entities

Due to the focus of entities being on their identity, it is very easy to fall into the trap of letting the database design dictate what your domain model will look like. This can lead to what is known as an **anemic domain model**.

Anemic models

Anemic models have little or no domain behavior as part of their design. This means that you are not getting the full benefit of DDD. In my experience, entities are where anemia shows up most often. It is quite easy to diagnose anemic models and course-correct them if they're identified early enough. If your model has mostly public getter and setter functions, no business logic, or depends on various clients to implement the business logic, you probably have an anemic model.

Here is what an anemic entity for our auction might look like:

```
package chapter3

import (
    "time"

    "github.com/Rhymond/go-money"
)

type AnemicAuction struct {
    id             int
    startingPrice  money.Money
    sellerID       int
    createdAt      time.Time
```

```go
    auctionStart   time.Time
    auctionEnd     time.Time
}

func (a *AnemicAuction) GetID() int {
    return a.id
}

func (a *AnemicAuction) StartingPrice() money.Money {
    return a.startingPrice
}

func (a *AnemicAuction) SetStartingPrice(startingPrice money.
Money) {
    a.startingPrice = startingPrice
}

func (a *AnemicAuction) GetSellerID() int {
    return a.sellerID
}

func (a *AnemicAuction) SetSellerID(sellerID int) {
    a.sellerID = sellerID
}

func (a *AnemicAuction) GetCreatedAt() time.Time {
    return a.createdAt
}

func (a *AnemicAuction) SetCreatedAt(createdAt time.Time) {
    a.createdAt = createdAt
}

func (a *AnemicAuction) GetAuctionStart() time.Time {
    return a.auctionStart
}
```

```
func (a *AnemicAuction) SetAuctionStart(auctionStart time.Time)
{
    a.auctionStart = auctionStart
}

func (a *AnemicAuction) GetAuctionEnd() time.Time {
    return a.auctionEnd
}

func (a *AnemicAuction) SetAuctionEnd(auctionEnd time.Time) {
    a.auctionEnd = auctionEnd
}
```

Please note that there is nothing necessarily wrong with this, and you will see a lot of Go code that looks like this. But you simply are not getting the full benefit of the domain-driven design if you do this. As you can see, any other construct that uses our AnemicAuction will potentially make assumptions about what some of our attributes are for. Furthermore, they will implement business logic themselves and may do this in different ways that our domain experts did not intend.

Let's refactor the code to the following:

```
package chapter3

import (
    "errors"
    "time"

    "github.com/Rhymond/go-money"
)

type AuctionRefactored struct {
    id             int
    startingPrice  money.Money
    sellerID       int
    createdAt      time.Time
    auctionStart   time.Time
    auctionEnd     time.Time
}
```

```go
func (a *AuctionRefactored) GetAuctionElapsedDuration() time.
Duration {
    return a.auctionStart.Sub(a.auctionEnd)
}


func (a *AuctionRefactored) GetAuctionEndTimeInUTC() time.Time
{
    return a.auctionEnd
}


func (a *AuctionRefactored) SetAuctionEnd(auctionEnd time.Time)
error {
    if err := a.validateTimeZone(auctionEnd); err != nil {
        return err
    }
    a.auctionEnd = auctionEnd
    return nil
}


func (a *AuctionRefactored) GetAuctionStartTimeInUTC() time.
Time {
    return a.auctionStart
}


func (a *AuctionRefactored)
SetAuctionStartTimeInUTC(auctionStart time.Time) error {
    if err := a.validateTimeZone(auctionStart); err != nil {
        return err
    }

    // in reality, we would likely persist this to a database
    a.auctionStart = auctionStart
    return nil
}


func (a *AuctionRefactored) GetId() int {
    return a.id
```

```go
}

func (a *AuctionRefactored) validateTimeZone(t time.Time) error
{
    tz, _ := t.Zone()
    if tz != time.UTC.String() {
        return errors.New("time zone must be UTC")
    }
    return nil
}
```

Even in our simple example, we can see the benefit of our entity having some business logic. We have guaranteed that time zones are consistent, made it clear to the caller that we only deal with UTC, and enforced this with errors. We have also given them a consistent definition of the elapsed duration of our auction, rather than depending on the consumer to define it themselves, which could potentially lead to drift.

So, why can't we use the same model for our database? As systems grow in complexity, you might find the need to store metadata about the auction, such as how many users viewed it, how effective ads were at pointing to this auction, or a tracing ID so that we can track a user's journey through the system. All this information is useful, but it does not belong in the domain model.

A note on object-relational mapping

Object-relational mappings (**ORMs**) are a popular approach to managing database persistence. They are not a DDD concept, but they are popular enough that I thought it was worth a brief mention.

For Golang, **GORM** (https://gorm.io) is a popular library for this. I am not a fan of ORMs – they lead to a layer of unnecessary abstraction and poor database query design, which is often one of the biggest reasons applications have performance issues. By using an ORM, you are delegating control of query creation and planning.

If you want to use an ORM, ensure it does not control how you write your entities in your DDD context; otherwise, you may end up with an anemic model. We also want to keep the coupling between our entity and ORM to a minimum. Therefore, I recommend you use an adaptor layer to decouple your ORM and DDD entity layer. We covered adaptor layers in more detail in the previous chapter.

Now that we understand entities, let's look at value objects.

Working with value objects

Value objects are, in some ways, the opposite of entities. With value objects, we want to assert that two objects are the same given their values. Value objects do not have identities and are often used in conjunction with entities and aggregates to enable us to build a rich model of our domain. We typically use them to measure, quantify, or describe something about our domain.

Before we go any further, let's write some Golang code to help us understand value objects a bit further.

Firstly, we will define a `Point` in the following code block:

```
package chapter3

type Point struct {
    x int
    y int
}

func NewPoint(x, y int) *Point {
    return &Point{
        x: x,
        y: y,
    }
}
```

We will also write the following test, which checks if two points with the same coordinates are equal:

```
package chapter3_test

import (
    "testing"

    "ddd-golang/chapter3"
)

func Test_Point(t *testing.T) {
    a := chapter3.NewPoint(1, 1)
    b := chapter3.NewPoint(1, 1)
    if a != b {
        t.Fatal("a and  b were not equal")
    }
}
```

To a human, these two points are, of course, equal. You visit point A or point B on a map; you will end up in the same place – that is, at coordinates 1,1. However, this test fails:

```
=== RUN    Test_Point
    value_objects_test.go:13: a and  b were not equal
--- FAIL: Test_Point (0.00s)
```

So, why does it fail? In Golang, when we use the & symbol, we create a pointer to a memory address where points A and B are stored. When we do an equality check, they are not equal, as A and B are stored in different memory locations.

Now, let's change our point definition to the following:

```
type Point struct {
    x int
    y int
}

func NewPoint(x, y int) Point {
    return Point{
        x: x,
        y: y,
    }
}
```

The test now passes (notice how we are no longer returning a pointer?). This is because the two points are now being compared on their values when we do an equality check. They are value objects; we can treat them equally if their values are equal.

Notice how, in the point class, x and y are lowercase? This is to stop them from being exported and mutated. It is recommended that value objects remain immutable to prevent any unexpected behavior.

Value objects should be replaceable. Imagine we are writing a game and using a point to represent the player's current location. We might write some code to *move* our player, as follows:

```
package chapter3

type Point struct {
    x int
    y int
}
```

```go
func NewPoint(x, y int) Point {
    return Point{
        x: x,
        y: y,
    }
}


const (
    directionUnknown = iota
    directionNorth
    directionSouth
    directionEast
    directionWest
)


func TrackPlayer() {
    currLocation := NewPoint(3, 4)
    currLocation = move(currLocation, directionNorth)
}


func move(currLocation Point, direction int) Point {
    switch direction {
    case directionNorth:
        return NewPoint(currLocation.x, currLocation.y+1)
    case directionSouth:
        return NewPoint(currLocation.x, currLocation.y-1)
    case directionEast:
        return NewPoint(currLocation.x+1, currLocation.y)
    case directionWest:
        return NewPoint(currLocation.x-1, currLocation.x)
    default:
        //do a barrel roll
    }
    return currLocation
}
```

The `point` here is a description of our player's location. We can take advantage of the replaceability of the value object to update the point representing a player's position to be a completely new value every time we move. In this specific instance, you'll also notice that the `move` function is side effect free. This is something we should strive toward as part of immutability.

By following the principles of immutability and side-effect-free functions, we have made our value objects easier to reason about and to write unit tests for. We can write very simple tests with multiple different inputs with predictable outputs. This will help us with the long-term maintenance of the system.

How should I decide whether to use an entity or value object?

We should aim to use value objects as much as possible when modeling our domain. This is because they are the safest constructs we can use when implemented correctly. We do not have to worry about consumers incorrectly modifying our instance in a way we did not intend.

If you care only about the values of an object, then it should preferably be a value object. Some other questions to ask yourself to ensure a value object is the right choice for you are:

- Is it possible for me to treat this object as immutable?

- Does it measure, quantify, or describe a domain concept?

- Can it be compared to other objects of the same type by its values?

If the answers to all these questions are yes, a value object is probably right for your use case.

At this point, it probably feels as if I am advising everything should be a value object. The truth is that this is not a bad way to think about it. Try and make everything a value object to start with until it does not fit your use case. At that point, it can be upgraded to an entity.

Now that we have a strong understanding of entities and value objects, we can build upon our knowledge and learn how to combine them with the aggregate pattern.

The aggregate pattern

Aggregates are probably one of the hardest patterns of domain-driven design and are, therefore, often implemented incorrectly. This isn't necessarily bad if it helps you organize your code, but in the worst case, it may hinder your development speed and cause inconsistencies.

In domain-driven design, the aggregate pattern refers to a group of domain objects that can be treated as one for some behaviors. Some examples of aggregate patterns are:

- **An order**: Typically, an order consists of individual items, but it is helpful to treat them as a single *thing* (an order) for some purposes within our system.

- **A team**: A team consists of many employees. In our system, we would likely have a domain object for employees, but grouping them and applying behaviors to them as a team would be helpful in situations such as organizing departments.

- **A wallet**: Typically, a wallet (even a virtual one) contains many cards and potential currencies for many countries and maybe even cryptocurrencies! We may want to track the value of the wallet over time and to do that, we may treat the wallet as an aggregate:

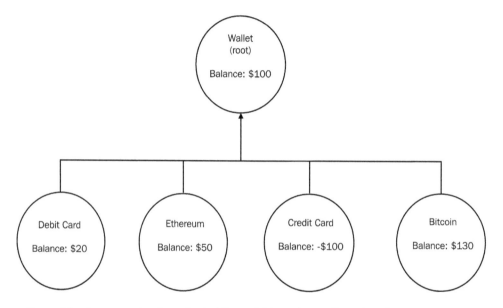

Figure 3.2 – An aggregate of a wallet holding a debit card, a credit card, and cryptocurrencies

Often, aggregates are confused with data structures used for collections of data, such as arrays, maps, and slices. These are not the same thing. While an aggregate may use these collections, an aggregate is a DDD concept and, therefore, will usually contain multiple collections, fields, functions, and methods. Instead, the job of an aggregate pattern is to act as a transaction boundary for the domain objects within. Loading, saving, editing, and deleting should happen to all objects within the aggregate or not at all. Let's look at our examples again:

- If an order is canceled, we should return all items within that order to stock. We may also want to trigger a refund.

- If a new employee joins a team, we may need to update the line manager structure.

- If a user adds a new card to their wallet, we need to ensure its balance is reflected in the total wallet balance.

Let's look at how we might implement the wallet aggregate we mentioned here:

```go
type WalletItem interface {
    GetBalance() (money.Money, error)
}

type Wallet struct {
    id uuid.UUID
    ownerID uuid.UUID
    walletItems []WalletItem
}

func (w Wallet) GetWalletBalance() (*money.Money, error) {
    var bal *money.Money
    for _, v := range w.walletItems {
        itemBal, err := v.GetBalance()
        if err != nil {
            return nil, errors.New("failed to get balance")
        }
        bal, err = bal.Add(&itemBal)
        if err != nil {
            return nil, errors.New("failed to increment balance")
        }
    }
    return bal, nil
}
```

Here are some interesting things to call out about this code block – id is our aggregate root and is our wallet's identity. OwnerID is the identity of the entity that owns the wallet. We do not always need to know all the details of an owner, but it gives us the ability to fetch them when necessary. walletItems is a collection of WalletItem. WalletItem is an entity we defined elsewhere, so for now, we just define an interface.

Discovering aggregates

One of the hardest tasks of domain-driven design is trying to discover which type of construct to use and when. Before trying to cluster our domain models into aggregates, we need to find our bounded context's *invariants*. An invariant is simply a rule in our domain that must always be true. For example, we may say that in our system, for an order to be created, we must have the item in stock. This is a business invariant. If we do not have an item in stock, we cannot promise it to customers.

For aggregates, we are looking for transactional consistency, not eventual consistency; we want any changes to our aggregate to be immediate and atomic. Therefore, we can think of an aggregate as a *transactional consistency boundary*. Whenever we make changes within our domain, we should ideally only modify one aggregate per transaction. If it is more, then your model is probably not quite correct, and you should revisit it.

Designing aggregates

Generally, we should aim for small aggregates. Keeping aggregates small will help make our system more scalable, improve performance, and give transactions more chance of success. Let's look at the order system again and imagine a multi-user scenario (that is, multiple customers are trying to order the same item from a website at once). We could model our order aggregate as follows:

```go
type item struct {
    name string
}
type Order struct {
    items            []item
    taxAmount        money.Money
    discount         money.Money
    paymentCardID    uuid.UUID
    customerID       uuid.UUID
    marketingOptIn   bool
}
```

This order struct seems reasonable and in line with what we see in many order flows online today. However, including marketing opt-in in this aggregate is a bad design for a couple of reasons:

- Firstly, from a bounded context perspective, marketing opt-in has nothing to do with the order object.

- Secondly, if a user were to opt out of marketing between starting an order and completing it, we would not want the order to not complete. Therefore, removing it from our aggregate makes sense:

```go
type Order struct {
    items            []item
    taxAmount        money.Money
    discount         money.Money
    paymentCardID    uuid.UUID
    customerID       uuid.UUID
}
```

> **Note**
> This does not mean we cannot include a marketing opt-in checkbox in our UI; it should just be decoupled from our aggregate and the transactional guarantee we want to achieve.

Aggregates beyond a single bounded context

Especially at the business scale, there will be situations where our bounded context changes and other sub-systems would like to be notified. Beyond our bounded context, we should expect (and aim for) eventual consistency. This means we expect the other systems to receive and process our event in a reasonable amount of time, but we do not expect it to be atomically up-to-date as we would expect our bounded contexts to be. This leads to more decoupled systems with stronger resilience and scalability possibilities. Check with the domain experts to see if eventual consistency is an acceptable trade-off to make room for these benefits. We will cover more about publishing domain events and microservices in *Part 2* of this book.

Summary

In this chapter, we learned about entities, value objects, and aggregates. We saw why they can be challenging to reason about and why they are probably the most important building blocks of domain-driven design.

By now, we understand the difference between value objects and entities and why value objects are much safer to use generally. Furthermore, we have learned how to use aggregates to ensure transaction boundaries, which is important in any system!

In the next chapter, *Chapter 4, Factories, Repositories, and Services*, we will cover the final core concepts of domain-driven design before we build some more complex applications together in *Part 2*!

Further reading

Take a look at the following resources to learn more about the topics that were covered in this chapter:

- *What is a UUID?*: `https://www.techtarget.com/searchapparchitecture/definition/UUID-Universal-Unique-Identifier`
- *What is Object-Relational Mapping?*: `https://www.techopedia.com/definition/24200/object-relational-mapping--orm`

4

Exploring Factories, Repositories, and Services

Factories, **repositories**, and **services** are the last major building blocks of **domain-driven design (DDD)** that we will learn about before bringing everything together in *Part 2* of this book, where we will build some services from scratch.

None of the factories, repositories or services are unique to DDD and are often used in projects not using the DDD approach. This makes them especially important and useful to learn about, as you will see them everywhere.

In this chapter, we will cover the following topics:

- The factory pattern – we will discuss what it is and when it is useful

- The repository pattern – we will walk through some examples to help you understand how they differ from database tables

- Services – we will look at domain services, application services, and infrastructure services and the difference between them all

By the end of this chapter, you will be able to understand factories, repositories, and services in the context of DDD as we explore these topics with the help of examples.

Technical requirements

In this chapter, we will write a small amount of Golang code. To be able to run it, you will need the following:

- **Golang**: You can find instructions to install it here: `https://go.dev/doc/install`. The following code was written with Go 1.19.3 installed, so anything later than this should be fine.

- **Text editor or IDE:** Some popular options are Visual Studio Code (`https://code.visualstudio.com/download`) or GoLand (`https://www.jetbrains.com/help/go/installation-guide.html`).

- **GitHub repository:** `https://github.com/PacktPublishing/Domain-Driven-Design-with-GoLang/tree/main/chapter4`.

Introducing the factory pattern

The factory pattern is typically used in object-oriented programming and is defined as an *object with the primary responsibility of creating other objects*. An example from PHP might look like the following:

```php
class Factory
{
    public static function build($carType)
    {
        if ($carType == "tesla") {
            return new Tesla();
        }

        if ($carType == "bmw") {
            return new BMW();
        }
    }
}


$myCar = Factory::build("tesla");
```

The factory class has a `static` method that accepts `carType` and returns a new instance. This is a very simple example, but we could also extend it to set sensible default properties on our `car` object. Typically, factory classes should have no other purpose than object creation.

While Golang is not an object-oriented language, the factory pattern is still useful. Here is the same example we discussed earlier, but this time in Golang:

```go
package chapter4

import (
    "errors"
    "log"
```

```go
)

type Car interface {
    BeepBeep()
}

type BMW struct {
    heatedSeatSubscriptionEnabled bool
}

func (B BMW) BeepBeep() {
    //TODO implement me
    panic("implement me")
}

type Tesla struct {
    autoPilotEnabled bool
}

func (t Tesla) BeepBeep() {
    //TODO implement me
    panic("implement me")
}

func BuildCar(carType string) (Car, error) {
    switch carType {
    case "bmw":
        return BMW{heatedSeatSubscriptionEnabled: true}, nil
    case "tesla":
        return Tesla{autoPilotEnabled: true}, nil
    default:
        return nil, errors.New("unknown car type")
    }
}
```

```go
func main() {
    myCar, err := BuildCar("tesla")
    if err != nil {
        log.Fatal(err)
    }
    // do something with myCar
}
```

In this example, we have created a very simple function that initializes some fields for us, making it very easy for the caller of `BuildCar` to use. We also have returned `error` if the car type is not valid.

Factories are a great way to standardize the creation of complex structs and can be useful as your application grows in complexity. Factories also provide encapsulation (that is, hiding the internal details of an object from the caller and only exposing the minimal interface they need). Finally, factories can help ensure business invariants are enforced at the time of object creation, which can dramatically simplify our domain model.

For example, if we were creating a booking system for a hair salon, and someone tried to create a booking outside of business hours, we might enforce this in our `CreateBooking` factory function as follows:

```go
package chapter4

import (
    "errors"
    "time"

    "github.com/google/uuid"
)

type Booking struct {
    id           uuid.UUID
    from         time.Time
    to           time.Time
    hairDresserID uuid.UUID
}

func CreateBooking(from, to time.Time, hairDresserID uuid.UUID)
(*Booking, error) {
    closingTime, _ := time.Parse(time.Kitchen, "17:00pm")
```

```
    if from.After(closingTime) {
        return nil, errors.New("no appointments after closing
time")
    }
    return &Booking{
        hairDresserID: uuid.New(),
        id:           uuid.New(),
        from:         from,
        to:           to,
    }, nil
}
```

The preceding example shows a factory function creating an entity. I have chosen to let the factory generate the ID. Let's explore entity factories a little bit more.

Entity factories

As we discussed in the previous chapter, entities have identities and they have a minimum set of requirements necessary to instantiate them. We should, therefore, ensure we create entities that satisfy this minimum set of requirements when we create them via a factory. If we want to set other properties, we can then provide other functions.

When designing an entity factory function, we need to decide whether we want the factory function to be responsible for generating the identity for our struct or whether we want to pass one as a parameter. Both ways are fine, but I tend to lean toward letting the factory function generate it unless you have a good reason not to.

Now we understand entity factories, let's look at repositories.

Implementing the repository pattern in Golang

Repositories are the parts of our code that contain the logic necessary to access data sources. A data source can be a wide variety of things, such as a file on disk, a spreadsheet, or an AWS S3 bucket, but in most projects, it is a database.

By using a repository layer, you can centralize common data access code and make your system more maintainable by decoupling from a specific database technology. For example, your company may have a desire to move from one cloud provider to another, and the database options are slightly different; perhaps one has a MySQL offering, and the other offers only the NoSQL databases. In this instance, we know we only need to rearchitect a small portion of our system (the repository layer) to be able to enable this change.

Some developers query the database using other channels (such as **Command and Query Responsibility Segregation** (**CQRS**), which we will discuss in *Part 2*). This can work, since queries should not change the state of the database, but if you are just starting, ensuring that all interactions with the database happen in the repository layer is recommended.

One mistake we often make with repository layers is to make one struct per database table. This should be avoided; instead, aim to make one struct per aggregate. The following diagram should help outline this:

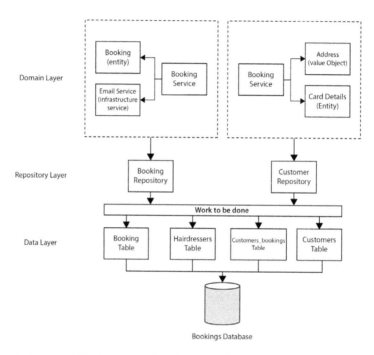

Figure 4.1 – How to think about repository layers and how other layers interact with them

Figure 4.1 shows a clear distinction between our database tables and our **repository layer**; a repository layer can write to multiple tables. Furthermore, our domain layer is decoupled from our repository layer. When we use DDD, we should always strive to build a system that looks like the one shown in *Figure 4.1*.

Let's continue with the booking system example from the previous section. We want to save our hair booking appointment to a database. We might define our interface as follows:

```
type BookingRepository interface {
    SaveBooking(ctx context.Context, booking Booking) error
    DeleteBooking(ctx context.Context, booking Booking) error
}
```

We define this interface in the same package as our `Booking` factory and our service layer (there will be more about services in the next section).

An implementation of a simple repository layer for a `Postgres` database might look like this:

```
type PostgresRepository struct {
    connPool *pgx.Conn
}


func NewPostgresRepository(ctx context.Context, dbConnString
string) (*PostgresRepository, error) {
    conn, err := pgx.Connect(ctx, dbConnString)
    if err != nil {
        return nil, fmt.Errorf("failed to connect to db: %w",
err)
    }
    defer conn.Close(ctx)

    return &PostgresRepository{connPool: conn}, nil
}


func (p PostgresRepository) SaveBooking(ctx context.Context,
booking Booking) error {
    _, err := p.connPool.Exec(
        ctx,
        "INSERT into bookings (id, from, to, hair_dresser_id)
VALUES ($1,$2,$3,$4)",
        booking.id.String(),
        booking.from.String(),
        booking.to.String(),
        booking.hairDresserID.String(),
    )
    if err != nil {
        return fmt.Errorf("failed to SaveBooking: %w", err)
    }
    return nil
}
```

```go
func (p PostgresRepository) DeleteBooking(ctx context.Context,
booking Booking) error {
    _, err := p.connPool.Exec(
        ctx,
        "DELETE from bookings WHERE id = $1",
        booking.id,
    )
    if err != nil {
        return fmt.Errorf("failed to DeleteBooking: %w", err)
    }
    return nil
}
```

As you can see, the interaction with the database is very simple, and there is no domain logic here; we would expect that to happen in the application service layer. Next, let's look at services and application services.

Understanding services

In DDD, we use a few different types of services to help us organize our code. These are application services, domain services, and infrastructure services. In this section, we will discuss all three services and when they are useful, starting with the domain service.

Domain services

Domain services are stateless operations within a domain that complete a certain activity. Sometimes, we will come across processes we cannot find a good way to model in an entity or value object; in these cases, it's a good idea to use a domain service.

It is particularly tricky to outline rules to use domain services; however, some things that you should look out for are the following:

- The code you are about to write performs a significant piece of business logic within one domain
- You are transforming one domain object into another
- You are taking the properties of two or more domain objects to calculate a value

Services should always be expressed using ubiquitous language from within the bounded context, just like everything else we do in DDD.

Let's look at a couple of examples of where a service can be helpful. Imagine we have the following pieces of code within our entities:

```go
package chapter4

type Product struct {
    ID              int
    InStock         bool
    InSomeonesCart  bool
}

func (p *Product) CanBeBought() bool {
    return p.InStock && !p.InSomeonesCart
}

type ShoppingCart struct {
    ID          int
    Products    []Product
    IsFull      bool
    MaxCartSize int
}

func (s *ShoppingCart) AddToCart(p Product) bool {
    if s.IsFull {
        return false
    }
    if p.CanBeBought() {
        s.Products = append(s.Products, p)
        return true
    }
    if s.MaxCartSize == len(s.Products) {
        s.IsFull = true
    }
    return true
}
```

The code looks reasonable at first, but it is problematic. While implementing `ShoppingCart`, we referenced another entity and added business logic, which does not really belong to `ShoppingCart`. To avoid this issue, we move the logic to a domain service, as follows:

```
package chapter4

import "errors"

type CheckoutService struct {
    shoppingCart *ShoppingCart
}

func NewCheckoutService(shoppingCart *ShoppingCart)
*CheckoutService {
    return &CheckoutService{shoppingCart: shoppingCart}
}

func (c CheckoutService) AddProductToBasket(p *Product) error {
    if c.shoppingCart.IsFull {
        return errors.New("cannot add to cart, its full")
    }
    if p.CanBeBought() {
        c.shoppingCart.Products = append(c.shoppingCart.Products,
*p)
        return nil
    }
    if c.shoppingCart.MaxCartSize == len(c.shoppingCart.
Products) {
        c.shoppingCart.IsFull = true
    }
    return nil
}
```

We now have a central place to house domain logic that spans two entities. This will become even more useful as we add more logic to `CheckoutService` that may use more entities (perhaps a discount entity or a shipping entity). Having this logic in a single-domain service means that if other clients want to implement our behavior, they can use our service, and our business invariants will be automatically enforced.

Domain services are perfect for when we need to compose domain logic in a stateless manner. However, if this doesn't fit our use case, we likely need an application service.

Application services

Application services are used to compose other services and repositories. They are responsible for managing transactional guarantees in place among various models. They should not contain domain logic (this belongs in the domain service, as discussed in the previous section).

Application services are usually very *thin*. They are used only for coordination, and all the other logic should be *pushed down* into the layers underneath the application layer. Typically, we also address security concerns in this layer.

An example in our booking context might look as follows:

```
package chapter4

import (
    "context"
    "errors"
    "fmt"

    "github.com/PacktPublishing/Domain-Driven-Design-with-
GoLang/chapter2"

)

type accountKey = int
const accountCtxKey = accountKey(1)

type BookingDomainService interface {
    CreateBooking(ctx context.Context, booking Booking) error
}

type BookingAppService struct {
    bookingRepo          BookingRepository
    bookingDomainService BookingDomainService
}
```

```go
func NewBookingAppService(bookingRepo BookingRepository,
bookingDomainService BookingDomainService) *BookingAppService {
    return &BookingAppService{bookingRepo: bookingRepo,
bookingDomainService: bookingDomainService}
}


func (b *BookingAppService) CreateBooking(ctx context.Context,
booking Booking) error {
    u, ok := ctx.Value(accountCtxKey).(*chapter2.Customer)
    if !ok {
        return errors.New("invalid customer")
    }

    if u.UserID() != booking.userID.String() {
        return errors.New("cannot create booking for other
users")
    }

    if err := b.bookingDomainService.CreateBooking(ctx,
booking); err != nil {
        return fmt.Errorf("could not create booking: %w", err)
    }

    if err := b.bookingRepo.SaveBooking(ctx, booking); err !=
nil {
        return fmt.Errorf("could not save booking: %w", err)
    }
    return nil
}
```

As you can see, we do some basic authorization checks and then compose our domain layer with our repository layer. In this specific instance, it would have been fine for our domain service to do the persistence too (since we do not cross any domain boundaries). By the end of this code block, we will have created and saved a new booking.

One other use case for application services is to power a **user interface** (**UI**). UIs may need to compose many different domain services, as demonstrated by the following flowchart. An application service can help us achieve this too.

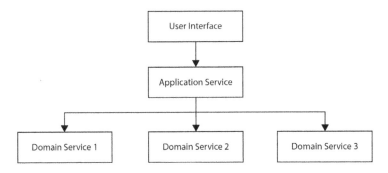

Figure 4.2 – A UI making use of application service

Figure 4.2 shows how a UI might use an application service to compose multiple different domain services to show a single screen to a user, with all the information.

Most modern web applications do the following:

- Accept payment (perhaps using Stripe or PayPal)
- Send email (perhaps using Amazon SES or Mailchimp)
- Track user behavior (perhaps using Mixpanel or Google Analytics)

None of these functions are part of our primary domain, but we still want to include them in our application. To do this, we can use an infrastructure service. This can then be added to your application service or domain service.

An implementation of an email infrastructure service might look as follows:

```
package chapter4

import (
    "bytes"
    "context"
    "encoding/json"
    "fmt"
    "net/http"
)

type EmailSender interface {
    SendEmail(ctx context.Context, to string, title string, body
string) error
```

```go
}

const emailURL = "https://mandrillapp.com/api/1.0/messages/
send\""

type MailChimp struct {
    apiKey     string
    from       string
    httpClient http.Client
}

type MailChimpReqBody struct {
    Key     string `json:"key"`
    Message struct {
        FromEmail string `json:"from_email"`
        Subject   string `json:"subject"`
        Text      string `json:"text"`
        To        []struct {
            Email string `json:"email"`
            Type  string `json:"type"`
        } `json:"to"`
    } `json:"message"`
}

func NewMailChimp(apiKey string, from string, httpClient http.
Client) *MailChimp {
    return &MailChimp{apiKey: apiKey, from: from, httpClient:
httpClient}
}

func (m MailChimp) SendEmail(ctx context.Context, to string,
title string, body string) error {
    bod := MailChimpReqBody{
        Key: m.apiKey,
        Message: struct {
            FromEmail string `json:"from_email"`
            Subject   string `json:"subject"`
            Text      string `json:"text"`
            To        []struct {
```

```
                    Email string `json:"email"`
                    Type   string `json:"type"`
                } `json:"to"`
        }{
            FromEmail: m.from,
            Subject:   title,
            Text:      body,
            To: []struct {
                Email string `json:"email"`
                Type   string `json:"type"`
            }{{Email: to, Type: "to"}},
        },
    }

    b, err := json.Marshal(bod)
    if err != nil {
        return fmt.Errorf("failed to marshall body: %w", err)
    }

    req, err := http.NewRequest(http.MethodPost, emailURL,
bytes.NewReader(b))
    if err != nil {
        return fmt.Errorf("failed to create request: %w", err)
    }

    if _, err := m.httpClient.Do(req); err != nil {
        return fmt.Errorf("failed to send email: %w", err)
    }
    return nil
}
```

We could then add it to our application service:

```
type BookingAppService struct {
    bookingRepo          BookingRepository
    bookingDomainService BookingDomainService
    emailService         EmailSender
}
...
```

Then, we could define a `CreateBooking` function as follows:

```go
func (b *BookingAppService) CreateBooking(ctx context.Context,
booking Booking) error {
    u, ok := ctx.Value(accountCtxKey).(*chapter2.Customer)
    if !ok {
        return errors.New("invalid customer")
    }

    if u.UserID() != booking.userID.String() {
        return errors.New("cannot create booking for other
users")
    }

    if err := b.bookingDomainService.CreateBooking(ctx,
booking); err != nil {
        return fmt.Errorf("could not create booking: %w", err)
    }

    if err := b.bookingRepo.SaveBooking(ctx, booking); err !=
nil {
        return fmt.Errorf("could not save booking: %w", err)
    }

    err := b.emailService.SendEmail(ctx, ...)
    if err != nil {
      // handle it.
    }

    return nil
}
...
```

As you can see, by the end of this code block, we have done the following:

- Created a booking
- Saved it to our database
- Sent an email to our customers to notify them about it

Summary

In this chapter, we learned about three different service types – application, domain, and infrastructure – and we saw some examples of what they might look like. We also learned about repository layers and their benefits. Finally, we looked at how we can use factories to simplify object creation as our application gets more complex.

This wraps up *Part 1* of this book. By now, you should have a preliminary understanding of all the concepts you need to implement a service using DDD. In *Part 2* of this book, we will put our new knowledge to good use as we build an entire service from scratch, using everything we have learned so far and a couple of new topics wherever relevant.

Part 2: Real -World Domain-Driven Design with Golang

In the second part of this book, we are going to learn how to apply DDD in a more real world setting and we are going to write a lot of Go code.

We will firstly look how we could apply DDD to both an existing and a new monolithic application. We will then move on to explore how we could build a microservice from scratch using DDD, whilst still ensuring we follow good resilience practices.

Finally, we will investigate how DDD can play a part in ensuring a large distributed system is organized and easy to reason about.

As a bonus, you can also enjoy a chapter on how we might use test-driven development and behavior-driven development alongside DDD.

This part comprises of the following chapters:

- *Chapter 5, Applying DDD to a Monolithic Application*
- *Chapter 6, Building a Microservice Using DDD*
- *Chapter 7, DDD for Distributed Systems*
- *Chapter 8, TDD, BDD, and DDD*

Applying Domain-Driven Design to a Monolithic Application

In the first part of this book, we learned about the theory behind **domain-driven design** (**DDD**) and looked at isolated examples of how we might implement each idea or pattern. In *Part 2* of this book, we are going to build real-world applications together that will help cement the ideas and give you example projects to reference in the future.

We will start by building a domain-driven monolithic application (after defining what a monolithic application is) from scratch. We will then discuss how you might apply DDD principles to an existing application that was not created using DDD from the beginning.

By the end of the chapter, you will be able to understand the following topics:

- What a monolithic application is, as well as in what situation you may want to build one
- How to build an entire domain-driven monolith from scratch
- How to identify that your existing application might benefit from applying domain-driven design

We'll get started by looking at what we mean by a monolithic application. But before that, let's go through the technical requirements of the chapter.

Technical requirements

In this chapter, we will write a large amount of Golang code. To be able to follow along, you will need the following:

- **Golang**: You can find instructions to install it at `https://go.dev/doc/install`. The code in this chapter was written with Go 1.19.3 installed, so anything later than this should be fine.

- **A text editor or IDE**: Some popular options are VS Code (`https://code.visualstudio.com/download`) or GoLand (`https://www.jetbrains.com/help/go/installation-guide.html`). All screenshots in this section are taken from GoLand.

- **GitHub repository**: All code for this section can be found here: `https://github.com/PacktPublishing/Domain-Driven-Design-with-GoLang/tree/main/chapter5`.

- **Docker**: We will use this to run a database on our machine. You can find instructions on how to install Docker here: `https://docs.docker.com/compose/install`.

> **A friendly warning**
>
> The application we are going to create in this chapter is intended for demonstration only and to really highlight how to work in the domain-driven design style. It is not production ready, and we will be skipping lots of best practices, such as testing and documentation. These are critically important but beyond the scope of this book.However, please see *Chapter 8* (P-Italics) for some insight on how testing and DDD can be complimentary

What do we mean when we say monolithic application?

A **monolithic application**, or **monolith**, is likely a term you have heard before, as it is probably the most popular pattern for developing an enterprise application. We call it a monolithic application if all the different components of the system are encapsulated into a single unit – for example, if the user interface, several domains, and infrastructure services are combined into a single deployable unit. The following figure illustrates this:

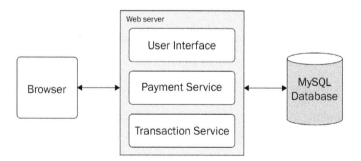

Figure 5.1 – Multiple services packed into a single application

Monolithic applications remain popular because of the following reasons:

- They are simple to develop. All code and concerns exist in a single place, and you do not need to worry as much about the failures that can come with remote procedure calls in distributed systems (more on this in the next chapter).

- They are simple to deploy. There is only one deployable, and its requirements should be well understood.

- They are simple to scale (to a point). Need more power? Simply deploy more versions of the application behind a load balancer.

However, there are also some major downsides. These downsides tend to appear as the application grows in complexity and/or scale:

- The startup time for the application can become multiple minutes. This quickly adds up to many hours wasted by engineers during development.

- Scaling the application starts to become difficult. In addition to the slow startup time, which can impact customers, monoliths can only typically scale in one dimension. And since the application covers so many different use cases, a lot of time can be spent optimizing configuration to cover all these use cases. This can lead to monoliths becoming very expensive on a resource front (for example, CPUs).

- Continuous deployment becomes slow. Even if you make a small code change to a specific part, you must deploy the entire application. This gets slower and slower as the application grows in complexity. Deployments taking longer than an hour are not unheard of.

- A long-term commitment to a specific technology stack is necessary. If your monolithic application is written in PHP, you must continue to use PHP, even if new application requirements would be better suited for new technology, or if you hire an expert in a different language – you have to stick with PHP. Moving to a new language would require a rewrite of the entire system (or parts of it if you decide to move to microservices. We will discuss microservices more in the next chapter).

- Changes become difficult to make. With the pressure of delivery and the barrier to beginning development getting higher, oftentimes, the modularity of the system can become blurred. This is where DDD can help!

In the next section, we will build a simple monolithic application using domain-driven design principles. Let's start by outlining the business for which we will build a system.

Setting the scene

In this section, we will outline a scenario using a fictitious company. Domain-driven design is all about solving business invariants in a specific context, and I hope this example will help reinforce that.

CoffeeCo is a national coffee shop chain. They experienced rapid growth in the last year and have opened 50 new stores. Each store sells coffee and coffee-related accessories, as well as store-specific drinks. Stores often have individual offers, but national marketing campaigns are often run, which influence the price of an item too.

CoffeeCo recently launched a loyalty program called CoffeeBux, which allows customers to get 1 free drink for every 10 they purchase. It doesn't matter which store they purchase a drink at or which they redeem it at.

CoffeeCo has been thinking of launching an online store. They are also considering a monthly subscription that allows purchasers to get unlimited coffee every month, as well as a discount on other drinks. Now that we understand the business domain, we can start to explore how we can build systems to help CoffeeCo achieve its goals!

We had a domain modeling session with the domain experts, which included employees at the coffee shop, people from the head office, and suppliers. In this session, we have identified the following ubiquitous language and definitions that we should keep in mind as we develop our system:

- **Coffee lovers**: What CoffeeCo calls its customers.

- **CoffeeBux**: This is the name of their loyalty program. Coffee lovers earn one CoffeeBux for each drink or accessory they purchase.

- **Tiny, medium, and massive**: The sizes of the drinks are in ascending order. Some drinks are only available in one size, others in all three. Everything on the menu fits into these categories.

During the domain modeling session, we identified the following domains:

- Store

- Products

- Loyalty

- Subscription

We will revisit each of these as we build our system.

We spoke about what would be a good **minimum viable product** (**MVP**) for the new system that we will create. The domain experts felt that the following features need to be in scope:

- Purchasing a drink or accessory using CoffeeBux

- Purchasing a drink or accessory with a debit/credit card

- Purchasing a drink or accessory with cash

- Earning CoffeeBux on purchases

- Store-specific (but not national) discounts

- We can assume all purchases are in USD for now; in the future, we need to support many currencies though

- Drinks only need to come in one size for now

Getting started with our CoffeeCo system

Now that we understand what our business does, let's begin to build a domain-driven system to satisfy all the requirements.

Let's start by initializing a new Golang project:

1. We will create a new project called `coffeeco` in our `Dev` folder using GoLand; you can use whichever IDE you like:

Figure 5.2 – Project creation screen in GoLand

2. Next, we will create an `internal` folder with a `loyalty` folder inside, as follows:

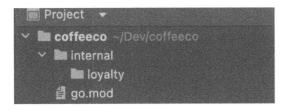

Figure 5.3 – Our project structure so far

The `internal` folder is a special folder in Golang. Anything within the `internal` directory cannot be imported by other projects. This is a great fit for DDD as we do not want our domain code to be part of our public API. To automatically enforce this, we will be putting all our domain code inside this `internal` folder.

3. Before we can write any code about the loyalty scheme, we need to define a few other structs. We know from the brief that the loyalty scheme is called CoffeeBux and that they can be collected at any store where a coffee lover purchases a drink. Therefore, let's start by defining a coffee lover.

    A coffee lover is most certainly an entity. This is because we want a coffee lover to be defined by their identity; whenever we are talking about a coffee lover and adding CoffeeBux to their loyalty account, there should be no doubt as to which coffee lover we are applying these.

    Let's create the `coffeelover.go` file inside the `internal` folder as follows:

Figure 5.4 – The coffeelover.go file

This will make it accessible to our entire domain code.

4. Inside `coffeelover.go`, we can add the following:

```go
package coffeeco

import "github.com/google/uuid"

type CoffeeLover struct {
    ID              uuid.UUID
    FirstName       string
    LastName        string
    EmailAddress    string
}
```

You'll notice that we have added some entity attributes (`FirstName`, `LastName`, and `EmailAddress`). This was after consulting the domain experts and understanding what information we need to store about coffee lovers. Domain-driven design is about constant communication with your stakeholders and it's essential you do this.

5. Next, let's add our `store` domain, as shown in the following figure:

Figure 5.5 – Adding a store domain

6. We create `store/store.go` in our `internal` folder and add the following code:

```
package store

import "github.com/google/uuid"

type Store struct {
    ID        uuid.UUID
    Location  string
}
```

Notice we have decided to make the store an entity again. Again, this is due to the fact that when we reference a store, it's really important that we can easily identify which one we are talking about.

This is a good start but a lot is missing that we have not defined yet. Each store sells coffee and coffee-related accessories, as well as store-specific drinks. We therefore need to define a product.

Defining products is our first real challenge. Should it be an entity or a value object? I think it could be either. Let's go back to our questions from *Chapter 3*:

*   Is it possible for me to treat this object as immutable?

*   Does it measure, quantify, or describe a domain concept?

*   Can it be compared to other objects of the same type just by its values?

We can answer *yes* to all of these questions. Furthermore, as we mentioned in *Chapter 3*, it is better to treat something as a value object and then *upgrade* it to an entity later, as it's a safer construct to deal with. Therefore, for now, we will treat the product as a value object. Let's go ahead and implement it:

1. We create the `product.go` file:

Figure 5.6 – The product.go file

2. Add the following code:

```
package coffeeco

import "github.com/Rhymond/go-money"

type Product struct {
    ItemName   string
    BasePrice  money.Money
}
```

We added the base price after consulting our domain experts. This is the language they use to refer to the non-offer price of a product. We should add this to our ubiquitous language definitions.

3. We can now go back to `store.go` and add our products:

```
package store

import (
    "github.com/google/uuid"

    coffeeco "coffeeco/internal"
```

```
)

type Store struct {
    ID              uuid.UUID
    Location        string
    ProductsForSale []coffeeco.Product
}
```

`store.go` looks pretty good. We now need to think of how we would like to model a purchase. This would be another situation we would speak to our domain experts about to understand the language they use to describe a customer buying coffee and whether there is anything surprising that we need to account for.

4. After a discussion, we create `purchase.go`:

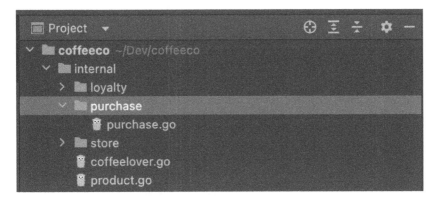

Figure 5.7 – Creating purchase.go

5. Then, write the following code:

```
package purchase

import (
    "github.com/Rhymond/go-money"
    "github.com/google/uuid"

    coffeeco "coffeeco/internal"
    "coffeeco/internal/store"
)
```

```
type Purchase struct {
    id                  uuid.UUID
    Store               store.Store
    ProductsToPurchase  []coffeeco.Product
    total               money.Money
    PaymentMeans        payment.Means
    timeOfPurchase      time.Time
}
```

Our `Purchase` type has its own ID and should be an entity; this makes sense. If a customer ever wants a refund on an item, we will need to be able to reference a specific transaction.

6. There is a little bit more we need to think about for a purchase. Did the customer use card or cash? If they used a card, which was it? We need to represent this behavior.

    We, therefore, need to make a payment domain. Let's create `payment/means.go`:

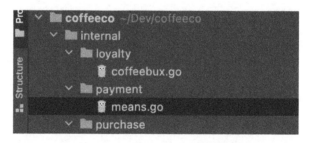

Figure 5.8 – Our project structure so far

7. And add the following code:

```
package payment

type Means string

const (
    MEANS_CARD     = "card"
    MEANS_CASH     = "cash"
    MEANS_COFFEEBUX = "coffeebux"
)


type CardDetails struct {
```

```
        cardToken string
    }
```

We have used a `type` alias here to represent payment means. We have also created a struct to represent `CardDetails`. This is not how card payments work, but in our simple example, we will assume we receive a token representing a card at the time of purchase, and that is what we will charge.

We have made some constants here to define cash and CoffeeBux payments too. This is a little pre-emptive, but we know we will need them shortly, so I see no harm.

8. Finally, we can go back and add the new `PaymentMeans` to `Purchase`:

```
type Purchase struct {
    id                  uuid.UUID
    Store               store.Store
    ProductsToPurchase  []coffeeco.Product
    total               money.Money
    PaymentMeans        payment.Means
    timeOfPurchase      time.Time
    CardToken           *string
}
```

9. We are nearly ready to add some service logic. However, first, let's define our loyalty scheme.

    Let's make `loyalty/coffeebux.go`:

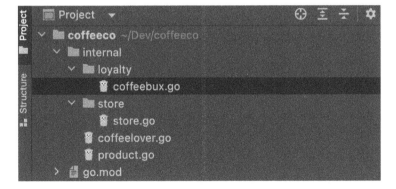

Figure 5.9 – Our project structure so far

10. `coffeebux.go` is going to contain the logic for the loyalty scheme. Let's add the following code:

```
package loyalty

import (
    "github.com/google/uuid"

    coffeeco "coffeeco/internal"
    "coffeeco/internal/store"
)

type CoffeeBux struct {
    ID                                   uuid.UUID
    store                                store.Store
    coffeeLover                          coffeeco.
CoffeeLover
    FreeDrinksAvailable                  int
    RemainingDrinkPurchasesUntilFreeDrink int
}
```

We reference a lot of other entities here. It really highlights why companies like having loyalty schemes; look at how much data we can gather!

We finally have all our domain models defined and we are ready to take our first pass at creating a service. A purchase is a good fit for service because of the following:

- We are about to perform a significant piece of business logic within our domain
- We need to calculate some values
- We need to interact with the repository layer

To program as defensively as possible, we are going to define a `validateAndEnrich` function in `product.go`. This will help us keep our service as thin as possible. Remember, we should always be trying to push down as much logic as possible into our domain objects:

1. Let's add the following code to `product.go`:

```
func (p *Purchase) validateAndEnrich() error {
    if len(p.ProductsToPurchase) == 0 {
        return errors.New("purchase must consist of at
least one product")
    }
```

```go
    p.total = *money.New(0, "USD")

    for _, v := range p.ProductsToPurchase {
        newTotal, _ := p.total.Add(&v.BasePrice)
        p.total = *newTotal
    }
    if p.total.IsZero() {
        return errors.New("likely mistake; purchase should
never be 0. Please validate")
    }

    p.id = uuid.New()
    p.timeOfPurchase = time.Now()

    return nil
}
```

In this code block, notice the following:

- Purchase is a pointer. That is because our function updates values that are missing.

- We initialize a total of 0 USD. We'd need to update this in the future to support more currencies.

2. Also, in purchase.go, let's add the following:

```go
type CardChargeService interface {
    ChargeCard(ctx context.Context, amount money.Money,
cardToken string) error
}
type Service struct {
    cardService  CardChargeService
    purchaseRepo Repository
}

func (s Service) CompletePurchase(ctx context.Context,
purchase *Purchase) error {
    if err := purchase.validateAndEnrich(); err != nil {
        return err
    }
    switch purchase.PaymentMeans {
```

```
    case payment.MEANS_CARD:
if err := s.cardService.ChargeCard(ctx, purchase.total,
*purchase.cardToken); err != nil {
        return errors.New("card charge failed,
cancelling purchase")
    }
    case payment.MEANS_CASH:
    // TODO: For the reader to add :)
    default:
        return errors.New("unknown payment type")
    }

    if err := s.purchaseRepo.Store(ctx, *purchase); err !=
nil {
        return errors.New("failed to store purchase")
    }
    return nil
}
```

The service is small. We call our `validateAndEnrich` function to mutate the `purchase` object for us to add some necessary values. We could also have made `Purchase` both a value object and an entity, which would have meant we did not need to mutate.

3. After calling `purchase.validateAndEnrich()`, we have some logic depending on the payment means. If it's a card, we call `CardService` to create the purchase. We don't have `CardService` defined yet, so for now, we are creating an interface.

Let's imagine that your team has split into two halves. One half is working on payments, and the other on implementing purchases. We could meet with the payment team and agree on a contract for what `CardService` will look like (in Go, we call these contracts *interfaces*), and then we can continue with our implementations at separate paces. This is a really powerful pattern so use it often when working with other teams!

Finally, if all goes well, we call `PurchaseRepo` to store our new purchase.

We define `repository.go` inside the `purchase` package:

Figure 5.10 – repository.go added to the purchase folder

And for now, it's just an interface:

```
package purchase

import "context"

type Repository interface {
    Store(ctx context.Context, purchase Purchase) error
}
```

Again, defining this as an interface is a good idea. As a team, we can now have a discussion about which database might be the best for this project and it has not slowed down development. We could satisfy this interface with any number of different databases.

We now have a basic outline of what our service will look like. We need to add an infrastructure service for payment and implementation of our repository layer. Let's do both now.

Implementing our product repository

After a discussion with the team, we have opted to use Mongo, a document database. The reason the team selected Mongo is that they have good experience with running it, and given that products and payments have flexible metadata, we think it will be a good fit.

From a development perspective, it also means we don't need to write any database migration scripts.

So, let's first connect to Mongo and then implement a product repository:

1. In `repository.go`, let's define a Mongo implementation. If you are going to have a lot of code or different implementations, you may want to store it in a different file. For now, I think it's fine in one:

    ```
    type MongoRepository struct {
        purchases *mongo.Collection
    }

    func NewMongoRepo(ctx context.Context, connectionString
    string) (*MongoRepository, error) {
        client, err := mongo.Connect(ctx, options.Client().
    ApplyURI(connectionString))
        if err != nil {
            return nil, fmt.Errorf("failed to create a mongo
    client: %w", err)
    ```

```
      }

      purchases := client.Database("coffeeco").
Collection("purchases")

      return &MongoRepository{
         purchases: purchases,
      }, nil
  }
```

2. Firstly, we define `MongoRepository` and write some basic code to connect. We return any errors. For this to work, you'll need to add two imports for the official Mongo Golang package. Therefore, your imports should now look like the following:

```
import (
    "context"
    "fmt"
    "time"

    "github.com/Rhymond/go-money"
    "github.com/google/uuid"
    "go.mongodb.org/mongo-driver/mongo"
    "go.mongodb.org/mongo-driver/mongo/options"

    coffeeco "coffeeco/internal"
    "coffeeco/internal/payment"
    "coffeeco/internal/store"
)
```

3. Now that we have the basic code to connect to Mongo, we need to satisfy the `Repository` interface we defined before. Let's do that:

```
func (mr *MongoRepository) Store(ctx context.Context,
purchase Purchase) error {
    mongoP := New(purchase)
    _, err := mr.purchases.InsertOne(ctx, mongoP)
    if err != nil {
```

```
        return fmt.Errorf("failed to persist purchase: %w",
    err)
    }
    return nil
}
```

4. Here, we also call a toMongoPurchase function:

```
type mongoPurchase struct {
    id                  uuid.UUID
    store               store.Store
    productsToPurchase  []coffeeco.Product
    total               money.Money
    paymentMeans        payment.Means
    timeOfPurchase      time.Time
    cardToken           *string
}

func toMongoPurchase(p Purchase) mongoPurchase {
    return mongoPurchase{
        id:                 p.id,
        store:              p.Store,
        productsToPurchase: p.ProductsToPurchase,
        total:              p.total,
        paymentMeans:       p.PaymentMeans,
        timeOfPurchase:     p.timeOfPurchase,
        cardToken:          p.cardToken,
    }
}
```

The reason we do this is to decouple our purchase aggregate from the Mongo implementation. We should also decouple all the other domain models from the database models, but I will leave that as an exercise for you.

For now, that's all we need. Our repository layer is very simple and lightweight, which is a sign that DDD is really helping us here.

Adding an infrastructure service for payment handling

For our payment service, we are going to use Stripe. Like our Mongo repository, we are going to decouple ourselves from Stripe as much as possible, as it is not part of our domain, and it is a tool that the company may change its mind on in the future. This can be particularly true for payment services if a cheaper option comes along.

So, here's how we connect Stripe from our service:

1. First, let's make `stripe.go` in our `payment` package:

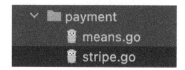

Figure 5.11 – stripe.go added to the payment folder

2. Next, let's add some basic code to initialize Stripe:

```go
package payment

import (
    "context"
    "errors"
    "fmt"

    "github.com/Rhymond/go-money"
    "github.com/stripe/stripe-go/v73"
    "github.com/stripe/stripe-go/v73/charge"
    "github.com/stripe/stripe-go/v73/client"
)

type StripeService struct {
    stripeClient *client.API
}

func NewStripeService(apiKey string) (*StripeService,
error) {
```

```
    if apiKey == "" {
        return nil, errors.New("API key cannot be nil ")
    }
    sc := &client.API{}
    sc.Init(apiKey, nil)
    return &StripeService{stripeClient: sc}, nil
}
```

Notice how we have imported the official Stripe package. You will need to add this to your go.mod.

3. Now that we have an initialized Stripe client, we need to satisfy the interface for CardChargeService. As a reminder, this is the interface:

```
type CardChargeService interface {
    ChargeCard(ctx context.Context, amount money.Money,
    cardToken string) error
}
```

We, therefore, implement that function on our StripeService struct:

```
func (s StripeService) ChargeCard(ctx context.Context,
amount money.Money, cardToken string) error {
    params := &stripe.ChargeParams{
        Amount:   stripe.Int64(amount.Amount()),
        Currency: stripe.String(string(stripe.
CurrencyUSD)),
        Source:   &stripe.PaymentSourceSourceParams{Token:
stripe.String(cardToken)},
    }
    _, err := charge.New(params)
    if err != nil {
        return fmt.Errorf("failed to create a charge:%w",
err)
    }
    return nil
}
```

This is near enough a copy and paste from the Stripe documentation (which is excellent). You can read more about creating charges in Stripe here: https://stripe.com/docs/api/charges/create?lang=go.

> **Challenge**
>
> See whether you can implement a different `CardChargeService`, perhaps using Square: `https://developer.squareup.com/gb/en/online-payment-apis`.

Now that we have done that, let's go back to our business requirements!

Paying with CoffeeBux

Our system is looking good! It is modular and easy to extend…so let's extend it.

As of now, we haven't satisfied all our business requirements. The requirements state that coffee lovers should get a coffee free after they have purchased 10 already. This means we need to track the number of purchases and also allow customers to pay with CoffeeBux. Let's design an entity to help us do this:

1. First, let's change our code so we are tracking free drinks. Let's add the following to `coffeebux.go`:

```go
func (c *CoffeeBux) AddStamp() {
    if c.RemainingDrinkPurchasesUntilFreeDrink == 1 {
        c.RemainingDrinkPurchasesUntilFreeDrink = 10
        c.FreeDrinksAvailable += 1
    } else {
        c.RemainingDrinkPurchasesUntilFreeDrink--
    }
}
```

This code checks whether we need to increment our free drink count and reset our purchased drinks counter. Otherwise, we just add a virtual *stamp*.

2. Now, let's go to `purchase.go` and update our `purchase` function to the following:

```go
func (s Service) CompletePurchase(ctx context.Context,
purchase *Purchase, coffeeBuxCard *loyalty.CoffeeBux)
error {
    if err := purchase.validateAndEnrich(); err != nil {
        return err
    }
    switch purchase.PaymentMeans {
    case payment.MEANS_CARD:
        if err := s.cardService.ChargeCard(ctx, purchase.
total, *purchase.cardToken); err != nil {
```

```
            return errors.New("card charge failed,
    cancelling purchase")
        }
    case payment.MEANS_CASH:
    // For the reader to add :)
    default:
        return errors.New("unknown payment type")
    }

    if err := s.purchaseRepo.Store(ctx, *purchase); err !=
    nil {
        return errors.New("failed to store purchase")
    }
    if coffeeBuxCard != nil {
        coffeeBuxCard.AddStamp()
    }
    return nil
}
```

Here, we have changed the signature of `CompletePurchase` to include `CoffeeBuxCard`. Notice how it's a pointer. This is because a customer is under no obligation to present a loyalty card and therefore, it can be `nil`.

At the bottom of our function, after a user has paid and they have persisted the purchase successfully, we add a stamp to their loyalty card. Notice how easy it was to add and how easy it is to follow our code?

3. We now need to add our loyalty card as a payment source. This is an interesting problem from a domain perspective because a loyalty card now belongs in both the `payment` and the `loyalty` domain. There are lots of different ways we could solve this problem and there is no wrong answer. The way we will solve it is to add CoffeeBux as a payment means. We actually already did this, and you can see it in `means.go`:

```
const (
    MEANS_CARD      = "card"
    MEANS_CASH      = "cash"
    MEANS_COFFEEBUX = "coffeebux"
)
```

4.   And in `loyalty.go`, we will add the following code:

```go
func (c *CoffeeBux) Pay(ctx context.Context, purchases []
purchase.Purchase) error {
    lp := len(purchases)
    if lp == 0 {
        return errors.New("nothing to buy")
    }

    if c.FreeDrinksAvailable < lp {
        return fmt.Errorf("not enough coffeeBux to cover
entire purchase. Have %d, need %d", len(purchases),
c.FreeDrinksAvailable)
    }

    c.FreeDrinksAvailable = c.FreeDrinksAvailable - lp
    return nil
}
```

In this code block, we program defensively and ensure that `purchases` is not empty. We then check there are enough free drinks to accommodate the entire purchase.

> **Note**
>
> We have made an assumption here that we should validate with the domain experts – it might be that they want to allow partial redemption of a purchase against a loyalty card. If that is so, our implementation is wrong, and we'd need to change it.

After this, we simply remove the necessary amount of free drinks from the CoffeeBux card.

We now have everything we need to accept payment in CoffeeBux, so let's go ahead and add it to `purchase.go`:

```go
func (s Service) CompletePurchase(ctx context.Context, purchase
*Purchase, coffeeBuxCard *loyalty.CoffeeBux) error {
    if err := purchase.validateAndEnrich(); err != nil {
        return err
    }
    switch purchase.PaymentMeans {
    case payment.MEANS_CARD:
```

```
        if err := s.cardService.ChargeCard(ctx, purchase.total,
*purchase.cardToken); err != nil {
            return errors.New("card charge failed, cancelling
purchase")
        }
    case payment.MEANS_CASH:
    // For the reader to add :)

    case payment.MEANS_COFFEEBUX:
        if err := coffeeBuxCard.Pay(ctx, purchase.
ProductsToPurchase); err != nil {
            return fmt.Errorf("failed to charge loyalty card: %w",
err)
        }
    default:
        return errors.New("unknown payment type")
    }

    if err := s.purchaseRepo.Store(ctx, *purchase); err != nil {
        return errors.New("failed to store purchase")
    }
    if coffeeBuxCard != nil {
        coffeeBuxCard.AddStamp()
    }
    return nil
}
```

We have added the ability to pay with your CoffeeBux card. However, there is a potential bug here. Can you spot it?

Right now, if you pay with your CoffeeBux card, you still earn a loyalty stamp. This is something we need to consult our domain experts about to see whether this is the correct business invariant.

We have one final feature to add to fulfill the project brief, which is to add store-specific discounts. Before we propose a solution in the next section, try and think about how you might approach it. Even better, try and implement it!

Adding store-specific discounts

First, we need to save store-specific discounts somewhere. We therefore need a repository layer:

1. Let's add `repository.go` to our `store` package:

Figure 5.12 – repository.go added to the store folder

2. And add the following code:

```go
package store

import (
    "context"
    "errors"
    "fmt"

    "github.com/google/uuid"
    "go.mongodb.org/mongo-driver/bson"
    "go.mongodb.org/mongo-driver/mongo"
    "go.mongodb.org/mongo-driver/mongo/options"
)

var ErrNoDiscount = errors.New("no discount for store")

type Repository interface {
    GetStoreDiscount(ctx context.Context, storeID uuid.
UUID) (int, error)
}

type MongoRepository struct {
    storeDiscounts *mongo.Collection
}
```

```go
func NewMongoRepo(ctx context.Context, connectionString
string) (*MongoRepository, error) {
    client, err := mongo.Connect(ctx, options.Client().
ApplyURI(connectionString))
    if err != nil {
        return nil, fmt.Errorf("failed to create a mongo
client: %w", err)
    }

    discounts := client.Database("coffeeco").
Collection("store_discounts")

    return &MongoRepository{
        storeDiscounts: discounts,
    }, nil
}

func (m MongoRepository) GetStoreDiscount(ctx context.
Context, storeID uuid.UUID) (float32, error) {

    var discount float32
    if err := m.storeDiscounts.FindOne(ctx,
bson.D{{"store_id", storeID.String()}}).
Decode(&discount); err != nil {
        if err == mongo.ErrNoDocuments {
            // This error means your query did not match any
documents.
            return 0, ErrNoDiscount
        }
        return 0, fmt.Errorf("failed to find discount for
store: %w", err)
    }
    return discount, nil
}
```

A lot of this code should look familiar from our previous repository layer. We may want to move some of the connection logic for a Mongo connection or pool of connections to a different package that we could share in the future.

When we use `GetStoreDiscount`, we check the error type; if it is `ErrNoDocuments`, we want to return a specific `ErrNoDiscount` error so that in the preceding layer, we know it's not a *real* error.

If all goes well, we simply return our store discount.

3. Let's make an interface for `StoreService` in `purchase.go`:

    ```
    type StoreService interface {
        GetStoreSpecificDiscount(ctx context.Context, storeID
    uuid.UUID) (float32, error)
    }
    ```

4. We will now add this interface to `PurchaseService`:

    ```
    type Service struct {
        cardService   CardChargeService
        purchaseRepo Repository
        storeService StoreService
    }
    ```

5. We then update our `CompletePurchase` function as follows:

    ```
    func (s Service) CompletePurchase(ctx context.Context,
    storeID uuid.UUID, purchase *Purchase, coffeeBuxCard
    *loyalty.CoffeeBux) error {
        if err := purchase.validateAndEnrich(); err != nil {
            return err
        }

        discount, err := s.storeService.
    GetStoreSpecificDiscount(ctx, storeID)
        if err != nil && err != store.ErrNoDiscount {
            return fmt.Errorf("failed to get discount: %w",
    err)
        }

        purchasePrice := purchase.total
        if discount > 0 {
            purchasePrice = *purchasePrice.Multiply(int64(100 -
    discount))
    ```

```
    }

    switch purchase.PaymentMeans {
    case payment.MEANS_CARD:
        if err := s.cardService.ChargeCard(ctx, purchase.
total, *purchase.cardToken); err != nil {
            return errors.New("card charge failed,
cancelling purchase")
        }
    case payment.MEANS_CASH:
    // For the reader to add :)

    case payment.MEANS_COFFEEBUX:
        if err := coffeeBuxCard.Pay(ctx, purchase.
ProductsToPurchase); err != nil {
            return fmt.Errorf("failed to charge loyalty
card: %w", err)
        }
    default:
        return errors.New("unknown payment type")
    }

    if err := s.purchaseRepo.Store(ctx, *purchase); err !=
nil {
        return errors.New("failed to store purchase")
    }
    if coffeeBuxCard != nil {
        coffeeBuxCard.AddStamp()
    }
    return nil
}
```

This is looking a little complex to read and isn't using a lot of domain-specific language in our service layer, so let's refactor a little:

```
func (s Service) CompletePurchase(ctx context.Context,
storeID uuid.UUID, purchase *Purchase, coffeeBuxCard
*loyalty.CoffeeBux) error {
    if err := purchase.validateAndEnrich(); err != nil {
```

```
        return err
    }

    if err := s.calculateStoreSpecificDiscount(ctx,
storeID, purchase); err != nil {
        return err
    }
    switch purchase.PaymentMeans {
    case payment.MEANS_CARD:
        if err := s.cardService.ChargeCard(ctx, purchase.
total, *purchase.cardToken); err != nil {
            return errors.New("card charge failed,
cancelling purchase")
        }
    case payment.MEANS_CASH:
    // For the reader to add :)

    case payment.MEANS_COFFEEBUX:
        if err := coffeeBuxCard.Pay(ctx, purchase.
ProductsToPurchase); err != nil {
            return fmt.Errorf("failed to charge loyatly
card: %w", err)
        }
    default:
        return errors.New("unknown payment type")
    }

    if err := s.purchaseRepo.Store(ctx, *purchase); err !=
nil {
        return errors.New("failed to store purchase")
    }
    if coffeeBuxCard != nil {
        coffeeBuxCard.AddStamp()
    }
    return nil
}
```

```go
func (s *Service) calculateStoreSpecificDiscount(ctx
context.Context, storeID uuid.UUID, purchase *Purchase)
error {
    discount, err := s.storeService.
GetStoreSpecificDiscount(ctx, storeID)
    if err != nil && err != store.ErrNoDiscount {
        return fmt.Errorf("failed to get discount: %w",
err)
    }

    purchasePrice := purchase.total
    if discount > 0 {
        purchase.total = *purchasePrice.Multiply(int64(100
- discount))
    }
    return nil
}
```

Here, we have added a `calculateStoreSpecificDiscount` function and updated our service layer. It is much cleaner now, and it will be easier to speak to our domain experts about it.

6. Finally, we need to implement `storeService` to satisfy the interface:

```go
type Service struct {
    repo Repository
}

func (s Service) GetStoreSpecificDiscount(ctx context.
Context, storeID uuid.UUID) (float32, error) {
    dis, err := s.repo.GetStoreDiscount(ctx, storeID)
    if err != nil {
        return 0, err
    }
    return float32(dis), nil
}
```

We have now written an entire service using the domain-driven concept. The finished package structure is as follows:

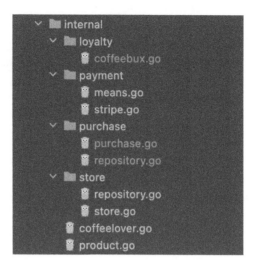

Figure 5.13 – The final package structure for our application

I have provided `main.go` to make it runnable and a `docker-compose` file in the GitHub repo here: `https://github.com/PacktPublishing/Domain-Driven-Design-with-GoLang/tree/main/chapter5`. This will enable you to run it and test it easily. In the README file, there are instructions on how to get it all started.

Extending our service

As an exercise, here are some features you might want to try and add to extend the service:

- Add an online store that allows customers to order a subscription
- Add drinks in different sizes
- Add unit tests
- Add an integration test

If you get them working, please feel free to create a PR into the example repo; I'd love to see them.

> **Applying DDD to an existing monolithic application**
>
> If you already work on a monolithic application, it is still worth trying to apply some of the patterns we have discussed throughout this book. My advice would be to start with building a strong relationship with the domain experts in your company. Together, you can start to build a ubiquitous language. If you start to reflect this in your code, you will notice that you will be able to start having much more meaningful and aligned conversations with them.
>
> It might be that moving to repositories and domain objects is too much of a refactor. That's okay. I would recommend that the infrastructure be the place where spending the time to decouple yourself from specific APIs (like we did with Stripe) is a valuable use of time. It will keep your business logic clearer and give the business more options when considering new providers in the future.

Summary

In this chapter, we got hands-on with Golang and built an entire application from scratch. We started by understanding the problem domain and building out a robust, ubiquitous language. We then built an application by splitting our application into domains, aggregates, repositories, services, and infrastructure services. Hopefully, you now see the true value of domain-driven design (if it was ever in doubt) and you are able to apply DDD principles to your own projects. In my experience, this is a highly desirable trait that is worth discussing when you are interviewing for new jobs.

In the next chapter, we will be looking at microservices, how they differ from monolithic applications, and what new things we need to consider when building them with domain-driven design in mind.

Further reading

* Stripe developer documentation: `https://stripe.com/docs`

* Using Go to connect to Mongo: `https://www.mongodb.com/docs/drivers/go/current/`

* What is a minimal viable product (MVP)?: `https://www.agilealliance.org/glossary/mvp/`

6

Building a Microservice Using DDD

In the previous chapter, we discussed how to build a monolithic application using **domain-driven design** (**DDD**). As your organization and code base scale, you may consider migrating to a microservice-based approach for development. To do this well, we need to use some DDD concepts we saw in the last chapter, but also some we did not. We know we are going to need to communicate with other microservices, and therefore we will be revisiting the anti-corruption layers, as well as ports and adaptors, that we learned about in *Chapter 2, Ubiquitous Language Bounded Contexts, Domains, and Sub-Domains.*

In this chapter, we will do the following:

- Learn what a microservice is, and how it differs from a monolithic application
- Learn at a high level when you and your company may benefit from considering a microservice-based architecture
- Build another service from scratch, using the ports and adaptor pattern, as well as the anti-corruption layer pattern

By the end of this chapter, we will have built an entire microservice from scratch that interacts with other microservices (accounting for failure scenarios) by using domain-driven principles.

Technical requirements

In this chapter, we will write a large amount of Golang code. To be able to follow along, you will need the following:

- Golang installed on your machine. You can find instructions to install it here: `https://go.dev/doc/install`. The code in this chapter was written with Go 1.19.3 installed, so anything later than this should be fine.

- Some sort of text editor or IDE. Some popular options are VS Code (`https://code.visualstudio.com/download`) or GoLand (`https://www.jetbrains.com/help/go/installation-guide.html`). All screenshots in this section are taken from GoLand.

- Access to GitHub. All code for this section can be found here: `https://github.com/PacktPublishing/Domain-Driven-Design-with-GoLang/tree/main/chapter6`.

- Docker installed. We will use this to run a database on our machine. You can find instructions on how to install Docker here: `https://docs.docker.com/compose/install`.

> **A friendly warning (again)**
>
> The application we are going to create in this chapter is intended for demonstration and to really highlight how to work in the DDD style. It is not production-ready, and we will be skipping lots of best practices such as testing and documentation. These are critically important, but beyond the scope of this book.
>
> Let's get started by looking at what a microservice is.

What do we mean by microservices?

Microservices, or microservice architecture, is a pattern of software development where teams build small services, with their own databases that communicate by some form of **Remote Procedure Call (RPC)**. Microservices are as much an organizational decision as they are a technical one; the goal is to make it as simple as possible to scale both teams and software.

The following diagram shows how an imaginary monolith might be split into microservices:

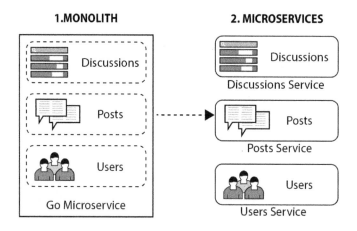

Figure 6.1 – A monolithic application split into three smaller services

Microservices typically exhibit the following characteristics:

- The service can be developed, deployed, and scaled independently; it should not impact the function of other services. It does not share code with other services, and communication with other services happens over some form of RPC.

- The service does not depend on other services being available to be successful. This does not necessarily mean it can do 100% of its function without another service being available, but it does mean another service crashing should not lead to our service crashing.

- The service solves a specific problem and solves it well. As the system grows more capabilities, it might be reconsidered to be broken into smaller microservices.

Microservices sound great! Let's look at their benefits in more detail.

What are the benefits of microservices?

The following are some of the key benefits of microservices:

- **Microservices enable teams to move fast**. Teams work and act within a small well-defined context and are empowered to make decisions themselves. This means the software development life cycle can be completed much quicker.

- **Flexible scaling**. Services can be scaled for their specific needs rather than just having one global configuration.

- **Easier deployments**. Since the code base is smaller and more focused, it is easier to build a deployment approach that suits your needs. Because it's faster, it also encourages and enables more experimentation as changes can be easily tested and rolled back.

- **Freedom to explore different technologies**. Using a different programming language or database is no problem in a microservice architecture.

- **More resilient.** Patterns can be adopted to ensure most of our architecture is available even when others are facing problems. We will explore this more in this chapter.

Up to now, we have made microservices sound like a silver bullet; they are not. They come with some major downsides. Let's look at these.

What are the downsides of microservices?

The following are the key drawbacks:

- Distributed systems require more expertise to manage than a monolithic architecture. Without much better visibility and tooling, you may see errors and issues that can appear "random".

- Engineers need to have a wider skillset than those who work on monolithic architectures. They may need to become familiar with platforms such as Kubernetes, and they need to think and care more about latency and networking.

- Testing user journeys can be much harder, especially in event-driven systems.

As you can see, microservices are not a free lunch, and their adoption needs to be considered carefully. Let's explore the adoption considerations together.

Should my company adopt microservices?

As with all technology initiatives, microservices come with trade-offs. What might be a great fit for one company might be a terrible fit for yours. Be sure to have a wide discussion with your team and be honest about the challenges ahead. Some questions you might want to answer:

- Do we have the expertise to run a distributed system? If not, what is our strategy to hire that expertise or train our staff?

- Do we have the necessary tooling in place to monitor a distributed system? If not, will we get the budget and time to put these in place?

- Which platform will we use to manage our distributed system? Kubernetes? Something else?

- How comfortable is our team with the said platform?

- How comfortable are our teams with building and owning their own CI/CD pipelines?

All these questions are basically lower-level questions that roll up to the ultimate question: will leadership invest the money and give us the time to do this?

Now that we understand the pros and cons of microservices, let's go ahead and build a microservice using DDD patterns and Golang!

Setting the scene (again)

You work for a travel comparison website. Your team is responsible for making recommendations on where a customer might be able to travel, given their budget and other factors. Your team is known internally as the recommendations team. Your team has been asked to expose your recommendations via an API so that other teams in the company may use it to build their own products.

There is another team in your company that is responsible for working with travel providers to onboard them and aggregate their costs and offer information to your system. They are known as the partnership team.

For your project, you are going to need to call the partnership system to gather information to allow you to create recommendations. The documentation for the partnership team is quite sparse, but thankfully the team has the following published details available on its team wiki:

```
"If you make a GET request to /
partnerships?location=$country&from=$date&to=$date we will
return all the hotels in that country on those dates.

$country must be in Alpha 3 ISO-3166 format and the date
must be ISO-8601 format. You can expect one of the following
responses:

400. This means you made a bad request, and your parameters
aren't in the correct format or were missing.

401. You are not authorized. You must pass an agreed password
in the Authorization header field"

200. This means your request was successful. You can expect the
following response:
{
    "availableHotels": [
    {
            "name": "hotel1_name",
        "priceInUSDPerNight": 500
    },
    {
        "name": "hotel2_name",
        "priceInUSDPerNight": 300
    }
    ]
}
There is no pagination, so if there are lots of hotels, the
response could be slow.


This API can be a little temperamental so fails sometimes; we
are not sure why. If you are going to call it, please prepare
for intermittent failure. Due to this, we are going to rebuild
the system soon, so don't recommend being too coupled to this
specific API. If it fails, you will receive a 500 response with
no body.
```

Although not in the OpenAPI format we discussed in *Chapter 2*, this documentation is succinct and helpful. It tells us everything we need to know and even gives us some reminders to implement patterns that will help us manage failures that may occur due to our system being distributed.

A few notes before we proceed:

- **ISO** is the **International Organization for Standardization**. It develops and publishes international standards for all sorts of things, including dates, currency codes, and times.

- *Alpha 3 ISO-3166* is one of the formats that they have defined, which outlines a three-character representation of each country. This standard is widely adopted and implemented in many libraries across many programming languages. By using this and being clear it is using it, the team had made an easy way for us to communicate our intention regarding our country to it without ambiguity. An example Alpha 3 ISO-3166 country code is **URK**, which represents **Ukraine**.

- *ISO-8601* is a format defined for timestamps. An example of this is 1969-01-14, which represents January 14, 1969.

We now know what we need to build and the other systems we need to talk to, so let's get started!

Building a recommendation system

To ensure we can focus on the important pieces of building a microservice using DDD principles, I have provided some sample code for this chapter. It's available here: `https://github.com/PacktPublishing/Domain-Driven-Design-with-GoLang/tree/main/chapter6`. In the repository, you will find an already completed Go program called `partnerships`. This is an API that gives back a response in the preceding format. However, to make it represent the system described previously, 30% of all requests will fail. You can run this program by running `docker-compose up`.

Once running, you can type the following into your terminal:

```
curl --location --request GET 'http://localhost:3031/
partnerships?location=UK'
```

If you do this a few times, you will notice you get one of two responses back. One is a 500 response, with no body. The other is this:

```
{
    "availableHotels": [
        {
            "name": "some hotel",
            "priceInUSDPerNight": 300
        },
```

```
    {
        "name": "some other hotel",
        "priceInUSDPerNight": 30
    },
    {
        "name": "some third hotel",
        "priceInUSDPerNight": 90
    },
    {
        "name": "some fourth hotel",
        "priceInUSDPerNight": 80
    }
  ]
}
```

We will use this API to develop our recommendation system.

Let's get started by creating a couple of folders, as shown in the following screenshot:

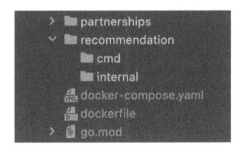

Figure 6.2 – Our folder structure so far

Here, we have made a new folder called recommendation. This will be the project's root. We have also made a cmd folder that is going to be the folder for our main binary, and an internal folder for our domain logic. This looks very similar to the service we started with in the previous chapter.

Inside internal, let's make another folder called recommendation and a file called recommendation.go. This is going to be where we write our domain recommendation service:

Figure 6.3 – Creation of recommendation.go

Let's add a domain model:

```go
type Recommendation struct {
    TripStart time.Time
    TripEnd   time.Time
    HotelName string
    Location  string
    TripPrice money.Money
}
```

Notice how we have used domain language again.

Next, we are going to define an interface for the partnerships system:

```go
type Option struct {
    HotelName    string
    Location     string
    PricePerNight money.Money
}



type AvailabilityGetter interface {
    GetAvailability(ctx context.Context, tripStart time.Time,
tripEnd time.Time, location string) ([]Option, error)
}
```

Notice here how we have not coupled our interface to the partnership's implementation at all. We have used domain language from our bounded context and defined what a reasonable, sensible interface is. This will help us a lot in the long run, as it will make moving to the new partnerships system much easier.

Let's create a service to house wrap this interface:

```
type Service struct {
    availability AvailabilityGetter
}


func NewService(availability AvailabilityGetter) (*Service,
error) {
    if availability == nil {
        return nil, errors.New("availability must not be nil")
    }
    return &Service{availability: availability}, nil
}
```

We have also created a `NewService` function that does some basic validation to ensure our service is in a good state before we use it.

Next, we are going to define a function called `Get` with the following signature:

```
func (svc *Service) Get(ctx context.Context, tripStart time.
Time, tripEnd time.Time, location string, budget money.Money)
(*Recommendation, error) {}
```

This function is in the `recommendation` package, so will be referred to as `recommendation.Get`, which makes clear what it does.

Let's implement some basic validation checks:

```
func (svc *Service) Get(ctx context.Context, tripStart time.
Time, tripEnd time.Time, location string, budget money.Money)
(*Recommendation, error) {
    switch {
    case tripStart.IsZero():
        return nil, errors.New("trip start cannot be empty")
    case tripEnd.IsZero():
        return nil, errors.New("trip end cannot be empty")
    case location == "":
        return nil, errors.New("location cannot be empty")
    }
    return nil, nil
}
```

From our domain rules, we know these cannot be empty, and it's always a good idea to validate.

Now we know that all our parameters are valid, we need to call the availability service:

```
opts, err := svc.availability.GetAvailability(ctx, tripStart,
tripEnd, location)
if err != nil {
    return nil, fmt.Errorf("error getting availability: %w",
err)
}
```

Note that we do not actually have a concrete implementation of this service yet and we do not know how it works. However, it does not stop us from developing our recommendation system.

Finally, let's do the calculation to make a recommendation:

```
tripDuration := math.Round(tripEnd.Sub(tripStart).Hours() / 24)
lowestPrice := money.NewFromFloat(999999999, "USD")

var cheapestTrip *Option
for _, option := range opts {
    price := option.PricePerNight.Multiply(int64(tripDuration))
    if ok, _ := price.GreaterThan(budget); ok {
        continue
    }
    if ok, _ := price.LessThan(lowestPrice); ok {
        lowestPrice = price
        cheapestTrip = &option
    }
}
if cheapestTrip == nil {
    return nil, errors.New("no trips within budget")
}
return &Recommendation{
    TripStart: tripStart,
    TripEnd:   tripEnd,
    HotelName: cheapestTrip.HotelName,
    Location:  cheapestTrip.Location,
    TripPrice: *lowestPrice,
}, nil
```

Here, we calculate the trip duration so that we can figure out if, given the price per night, we can find a trip within budget. We then loop through all the options we got back from our availability service, skipping any that are outside of the budget. Finally, we return an error if there is none within budget, and a recommendation for the cheapest if there were several. This is a small service, and it has used lots of language from our bounded context.

Let's take a closer look at the `AvailabilityGetter` interface and the DDD adaptor pattern.

Revisiting the anti-corruption layer

We looked at the anti-corruption layer (also known as the adapter pattern) in *Chapter 2*. As a reminder, the adaptor pattern is useful for decoupling two different bounded contexts from each other, which helps separate concerns and ensure our systems can evolve independently and safely.

Let's add an adaptor layer that satisfies the `AvailabilityGetter` interface.

Firstly, let's make a new file called `adapter.go`:

Figure 6.4 – Creation of adapter.go

Firstly, let's define a client struct and a New function:

```go
type PartnershipAdaptor struct {
    client *http.Client
    url    string
}


func NewPartnerShipAdaptor(client *http.Client, url string)
(*Client, error) {
    if client == nil {
        return nil, errors.New("client cannot be nil")
    }
    if url == "" {
        return nil, errors.New("url cannot be empty")
```

```
    }

    return &Client{client: client, url: url}, nil
}
```

This is a pattern we have used throughout the book; we are simply validating that nothing we expect to not be empty or nil is.

Next, we want our adaptor to satisfy the `AvailabilityGetter` interface. This means we need to add the `GetAvailability` function to the client. Let's stub that out:

```
func (p PartnershipAdaptor) GetAvailability(ctx context.
Context, tripStart time.Time, tripEnd time.Time, location
string) ([]Option, error) {

    return nil,nil
}
```

Great! Let's start implementing it:

```
from := fmt.Sprintf("%d-%d-%d", tripStart.Year(), tripStart.
Month(), tripStart.Day())
to := fmt.Sprintf("%d-%d-%d", tripEnd.Year(), tripEnd.Month(),
tripEnd.Day())

url := fmt.Sprintf("%s/partnerships?location=%s&from=%s&to=%s",
p.url, location, from, to)
res, err := p.client.Get(url)
if err != nil {
    return nil, fmt.Errorf("failed to call partnerships: %w",
err)
}
defer res.Body.Close()
if res.StatusCode != http.StatusOK {
    return nil, fmt.Errorf("bad request to partnerships: %d",
res.StatusCode)
}
```

Firstly, we make a GET call to the partnership endpoint using the client we have passed in. We will revisit this later to talk about how to ensure this is more resilient.

Assuming this is successful, we want to access the response. Therefore, we need to define what that response looks like as a Golang struct. We know what the response looks like from the partnership team's documentation, so we can define it as follows:

```
type partnerShipsResponse struct {
    AvailableHotels []struct {
        Name                string `json:"name"`
        PriceInUSDPerNight int    `json:"priceInUSDPerNight"`
    } `json:"availableHotels"`
}
```

We can now decode the response from the request into this struct:

```
var pr partnerShipsResponse
if err := json.NewDecoder(res.Body).Decode(&pr); err != nil {
    return nil, fmt.Errorf("could not decode the response body
of partnerships: %w", err)
}
```

Finally, we need to convert the response from the partnerships' structure into our required []Options:

```
opts := make([]Option, len(pr.AvailableHotels))
for i, p := range pr.AvailableHotels {
    opts[i] = Option{
        HotelName:    p.Name,
        Location:     location,
        PricePerNight: *money.New(int64(p.PriceInUSDPerNight),
"USD"),
    }
}
return opts, nil
```

Since we know the response size, we can make an array of the exact size we need and fill it as we iterate over AvailableHotels.

The entire function, therefore, looks like this:

```
func (p PartnershipAdaptor) GetAvailability(ctx context.
Context, tripStart time.Time, tripEnd time.Time, location
string) ([]Option, error) {
```

```go
    res, err := p.client.Get(fmt.Sprintf("%s/
partnerships?location=%s?from=%s?to=%s ", p.url, location,
tripStart, tripEnd))
    if err != nil {
        return nil, fmt.Errorf("failed to call partnerships: %w",
err)
    }
    defer res.Body.Close()
    var pr partnerShipsResponse
    if err := json.NewDecoder(res.Body).Decode(&pr); err != nil
{
        return nil, fmt.Errorf("could not decode the response
body of partnerships: %w", err)
    }


    opts := make([]Option, len(pr.AvailableHotels))
    for i, p := range pr.AvailableHotels {
        opts[i] = Option{
            HotelName:      p.Name,
            Location:       location,
            PricePerNight:  *money.New(int64(p.PriceInUSDPerNight),
"USD"),
        }
    }
    return opts, nil
}
```

This is everything we need for our adapter layer (apart from testing it rigorously, of course).

Exposing our service via an open host service

We have a requirement that our service must also expose an API. This is so other microservices or user interfaces may call us to get a recommendation. One method we could use to do this is to generate an API using OpenAPI or gRPC, as we discussed in *Chapter 2*. However, for completeness, we are going to write this one from scratch.

Let's define a contract first. We are going to create an API that receives the following request:

```
/recommendation?location=$country?from=$date&to=$date&budget
=$budget
```

It returns the following response:

```
{

    "hotelName": "hotel Name",
    "totalCost": {
    "cost": 300,
    "currency": "USD"
    }
}
```

Notice how the response we intend to return is different from the partnership system? This is completely normal. We own our domain, and as such, we can decide on requests/responses that make sense given the use case of our system. Typically, we will work with teams that will be calling our service to ensure we are returning something that is reasonable for their use case, but also makes sense for our API to return.

Now we have a contract, let's go ahead and define an HTTP handler. Firstly, let's define the following:

```
type Handler struct {
    svc Service
}

func NewHandler(svc Service) (*Handler, error) {
    if svc == (Service{}) {
        return nil, errors.New("service cannot be empty")
    }
    return &Handler{svc: svc}, nil
}
```

In the preceding code, we define a `Handler` struct and a `New` function that does some basic validation to ensure it's not empty. We will need the `Service` shortly since our `Handler` function is just a means to expose our business logic, and our business logic lives on our `Service`.

Next, let's define a struct that matches the contract we created previously:

```
type GetRecommendationResponse struct {
    HotelName string `json:"hotelName"`
    TotalCost struct {
        Cost     int64  `json:"cost"`
        Currency string `json:"currency"`
    } `json:"totalCost"`
}
```

We will use this shortly to marshal/unmarshal our response from Golang to JSON.

Finally, we can define our actual `Handler` function. Let's do it in stages since it's quite verbose:

```go
func (h Handler) GetRecommendation(w http.ResponseWriter, req
*http.Request) {
    q := mux.Vars(req)
    location, ok := q["location"]
    if !ok {
        w.WriteHeader(http.StatusBadRequest)
        return
    }
    from, ok := q["from"]
    if !ok {
        w.WriteHeader(http.StatusBadRequest)
        return
    }
    to, ok := q["to"]
    if !ok {
        w.WriteHeader(http.StatusBadRequest)
        return
    }
    budget, ok := q["budget"]
    if !ok {
        w.WriteHeader(http.StatusBadRequest)
        return
    }
}
```

`GetRecomendation` matches the criteria for a `Handler` function. This will be important in a moment because it means we can register it on an HTTP router, and therefore we'll be able to expose it to the outside world for others to call it.

We are using the `github.com/gorilla/mux` package to extract all the expectation query strings from our request and check they are not empty. If any of them are, we return a bad request response. This serves as another adaptor layer and protects our business logic from receiving requests that will never succeed due to missing pre-requisite information:

```go
const expectedFormat = "2006-01-02"


formattedStart, err := time.Parse(expectedFormat, from)
```

```
if err != nil {
    w.WriteHeader(http.StatusBadRequest)
    return
}
formattedEnd, err := time.Parse(expectedFormat, to)
if err != nil {
    w.WriteHeader(http.StatusBadRequest)
    return
}
```

The next thing we do is transform the dates we received on the request into a format that our service expects and return a bad request if we cannot. Again, this allows us to "fail fast" if we know the requests can never succeed due to not being of the right type or in the right format:

```
b, err := strconv.ParseInt(budget, 10, 64)
if err != nil {
    w.WriteHeader(http.StatusBadRequest)
    return
}
budgetMon := money.New(b, "USD")
```

We do the same thing for the budget. Our server expects the budget to be of a money type, but it is currently a string. We need to convert it. For now, we assume all requests are USD, but this is something we would need to improve in the future:

```
rec, err := h.svc.Get(req.Context(), formattedStart,
formattedEnd, location, budgetMon)
if err != nil {
    w.WriteHeader(http.StatusInternalServerError)
    return
}

res, err := json.Marshal(GetRecommendationResponse{
    HotelName: rec.HotelName,
    TotalCost: struct {
        Cost     int64  `json:"cost"`
        Currency string `json:"currency"`
    }{
        Cost:      rec.TripPrice.Amount(),
```

```
      Currency: "USD",
   },
})
if err != nil {
   w.WriteHeader(http.StatusInternalServerError)
   return
}
w.WriteHeader(http.StatusOK)
_, _ = w.Write(res)
return
```

Finally, we call our service. If we receive an error from the service, we return an internal server error since something must have gone wrong that we did not expect. If it does succeed, we marshal our response into our expected response format and return it.

Our open host service is looking good! We mentioned previously that we used an `http.handler` function type to enable us to "attach" it to a router. Let's have a look at how we might do that.

Firstly, we are going to make an entirely new package called `transport` and a file called `transporthttp.go`:

Figure 6.5 – Creation of transporthttp.go

This is a nice way to decouple the more specific implementation of transport types from your domain code. The `transporthttp.go` file is fairly simple and looks like this:

```
package transport

import (
   "net/http"

   "github.com/gorilla/mux"

   "github.com/PacktPublishing/Domain-Driven-Design-with-
GoLang/chapter6/recommendation/internal/recommendation"
)
```

```
func NewMux(recHandler recommendation.Handler) *mux.Router {
    m := mux.NewRouter()
    m.HandleFunc("/recommendation", recHandler.
GetRecommendation).Methods(http.MethodGet)
    return m
}
```

We again use the `gorilla/mux` package to make it easy to create a router, and we connect our service to the `/recommendation` endpoint. That's it!

We have an entire microservice now. The only thing left to do is to write a `main.go` file to put everything to get it so that we can run it. Let's do that now.

In the `recommendation` root folder, we create a `cmd` folder and a `main.go` file:

Figure 6.6 – Creation of main.go

In `main.go`, we write the `main` function. Let's step through it:

```
package main

import (
    "log"
    "net/http"

    "github.com/hashicorp/go-retryablehttp"

    "github.com/PacktPublishing/Domain-Driven-Design-with-
GoLang/chapter6/recommendation/internal/recommendation"
    "github.com/PacktPublishing/Domain-Driven-Design-with-
GoLang/chapter6/recommendation/internal/transport"
)

func main() {
    c := retryablehttp.NewClient()
    c.RetryMax = 10
```

Firstly, we create a `retryablehttp` client using a library provided by HashiCorp. This enables us to configure a retry policy that determines how we handle 5xx errors. This is helpful in our case as we know the partnership service can and will fail regularly. This is an important lesson to always keep in mind when working on distributed systems; we should always expect failure and account for it in our programming:

```
partnerAdaptor, err := recommendation.NewPartnerShipAdaptor(
    c.StandardClient(),
    "http://localhost:3031",
)
if err != nil {
    log.Fatal("failed to create a partnerAdaptor: ", err)
}
```

Next, we create a `partnerAdaptor`. Our `NewPartnerShipAdaptor` takes an `*http.StandardClient`, so we need to convert our `retryablehttp` client to that. Thankfully, the library provides an easy means to do that. We also must provide a base URL for our partnership service. Here, we have hardcoded the URL that our partnership system runs on if we do `docker-compose up`. You may want to move this to be an environment variable:

```
svc, err := recommendation.NewService(partnerAdaptor)
if err != nil {
    log.Fatal("failed to create a service: ", err)
}


handler, err := recommendation.NewHandler(*svc)
if err != nil {
    log.Fatal("failed to create a handler: ", err)
}
```

Next, we make a new service and a new handler. If for any reason we cannot create either, we call `log.Fatal`, which shuts down the program immediately. This is because there is no point in proceeding as our basic pre-requisite conditions are not met:

```
m := transport.NewMux(*handler)

if err := http.ListenAndServe(":4040", m); err != nil {
    log.Fatal("server errored: ", err)
}
```

Finally, we create a server and expose it on port 4040. We now have a microservice ready to run! You can run it by typing go run recommendation/cmd/main.go into your terminal.

Assuming you still have the Docker image running from before, you should be able to run the following command in your terminal:

```
curl --location --request GET 'http://localhost:4040/recommenda
tion?location=UK&from=2022-09-01&to=2022-09-08&budget=5000'
```

After running it, you'll see the following response:

```
{
    "hotelName": "some fourth hotel",
    "totalCost": {
        "cost": 210,
        "currency": "USD"
    }
}
```

Due to our retryablehttp client, even when the partnerships' service returns an error, we do not see it as it is retried automatically.

Summary

In this chapter, we have discussed the pros and cons of building microservices and seen how domain-driven patterns such as the domain model, the anti-corruption layer, and the open host service can help us to build maintainable microservices. We also discussed how we should expect failure and how we could use simple patterns such as retryable HTTP calls to make our system resilient to these failures.

In the next (and final) chapter, we are going to dig deeper into distributed systems and explore some more advanced DDD patterns that we can use to make our system simpler to reason about, easier to maintain, and—perhaps most importantly—easy to add new functionality to.

7

DDD for Distributed Systems

In the previous chapter, we built a microservice from scratch. The microservice we built communicated with another microservice in a synchronous fashion to attain some data to allow it to fulfill a business requirement. In this chapter, we are going to explore some other patterns for how microservices might communicate and share data as part of a larger distributed system. We will cover some patterns that have become synonymous with **domain-driven design** (**DDD**), such as **Command and Query Responsibility Segregation** (**CQRS**) and **event-driven architecture** (**EDA**). However, we will also cover some general distributed system concepts such as message buses and resilient patterns. These are not strictly domain-driven concepts but are complementary nonetheless and are certainly useful.

By the end of this chapter, you will be able to answer the following questions:

- What do we mean by a distributed system?
- What are CQRS and EDA?
- What is event sourcing?
- What is a message bus?
- How can we best deal with failure?

Let's get started.

Technical requirements

In this chapter, we will write some Golang code. To be able to follow along, you will need:

- Golang installed on your machine. You can find instructions to install it here: `https://go.dev/doc/install`. The code in this chapter was written with Go 1.19.3 installed, so anything later than this should be fine.

- Some sort of text editor or IDE. Some popular options are VS Code (`https://code.visualstudio.com/download`) or GoLand (`https://www.jetbrains.com/help/go/installation-guide.html`). All screenshots in this chapter are taken from GoLand.

- Access to GitHub. All code for this chapter can be found here: `https://github.com/PacktPublishing/Domain-Driven-Design-with-GoLang/tree/main/chapter7`.

What is a distributed system?

A distributed system is characterized as various computing components that are spread out over a network. These devices will coordinate to complete tasks that are more efficient/not possible if a single computer were to try to achieve them. Here's a visual example of a distributed system:

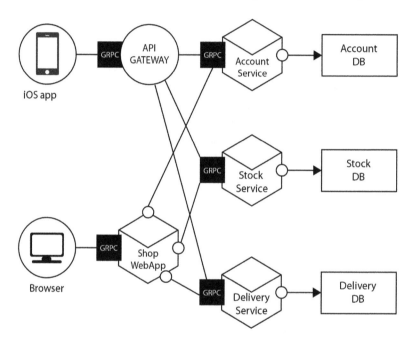

Figure 7.1 – An example of a distributed system

Distributed systems have grown in complexity over the years, but paradoxically there has never been a better time to build and run one. Due to cloud companies such as **Amazon Web Services** (**AWS**), Cloudflare, and DigitalOcean, getting started with complex systems is available to anyone for free where there used to be a very high barrier to entry.

A distributed system usually has the following characteristics:

- **Scalable**: The system can grow as workloads increase. For example, if your customers are heavily based in the United States, you may see large traffic between 9 A.M. and 5 P.M. in the daytime, but low traffic in the evening. You may choose to scale up and down your system to match these patterns and optimize for costs.

- **Fault-tolerant**: If one piece of our system fails, it shouldn't all fail. Imagine you are trying to pay for a product on a website and it keeps saying **Oops, something went wrong, please try again later**; however, the rest of the site remains fully functional. You can add things to your basket, browse other products, and leave reviews. This is fault tolerance at work; the payment system being down does not take the rest of the sit-down.

- **Transparent**: Our system appears as a single unit to our end users; they do not need to worry about the underlying implementation.

- **Concurrent**: Multiple activities can happen at the same time within our system.

- **Heterogenous**: This is a fancy word that means we can use a variety of servers, programming languages, and paradigms. For example, we may run some servers using Windows, and some using Linux. Some parts of our system may run in Kubernetes, while some might run on Raspberry Pi. Some of the systems may use an event-driven model and some might be synchronous. Some engineers may use Golang and some Python.

- **Replicated**: Information is often replicated to enable fault tolerance. For example, one common pattern is to have a primary Postgres database and a secondary read-only version that is replicated from the primary for redundancy.

You often must make trade-offs in the preceding categories to build a distributed system. A famous theorem taught in computer science classes is called the **CAP theorem**. The CAP theorem states you must pick two of the following categories to make guarantees about, and the third you must accept will suffer. These are:

- **Consistency**: Every read receives the most up-to-date information or an error.

- **Availability**: Every request receives a non-error response, but it may not receive the most up-to-date information.

- **Partition tolerance**: The system continues to operate even if there are network issues happening (such as packets being dropped). In the event of a failure here, the system designer must make a choice between:

  - Canceling the operation and thus decreasing the availability but ensuring consistency

  - Proceeding with the operation and thus providing availability but risking inconsistency

Let's look at one useful application for the CAP theorem: choosing a database for our system.

CAP theorem and databases

You'll often see CAP theorem trade-offs used for describing databases. For example, Mongo is a popular NoSQL database. Mongo is described as a CP database. This means it delivers consistency and partition tolerance, but it does so at the expense of availability.

Mongo has a single primary node. This node must receive all write operations. Once persisted, these new writes are replicated to secondary nodes. By default, clients read from the primary node to ensure they get the most recent information, but they can also read from a secondary node if configured to do so.

If the primary goes down, a secondary with the most recent data is promoted. The database is unavailable at this time. Once all the secondaries catch up, the database system becomes available again. Here is a diagram of how replication works in a Mongo cluster:

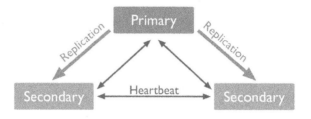

Figure 7.2 – Mongo replication

Alternatively, Cassandra is an AP database. Cassandra prioritizes availability and partition tolerance but sacrifices consistency. Cassandra has no primary, and you can write to any of the nodes. Cassandra claims that it can survive the complete loss of a data center and has no **single point of failure** (**SPOF**) due to all the nodes being the same. You can also scale out Cassandra horizontally as it uses something called "consistent hashing". In consistent hashing, keys are distributed in an abstract hash ring that is not dependent on the number of nodes we currently have. A simplified example of how this works is provided here:

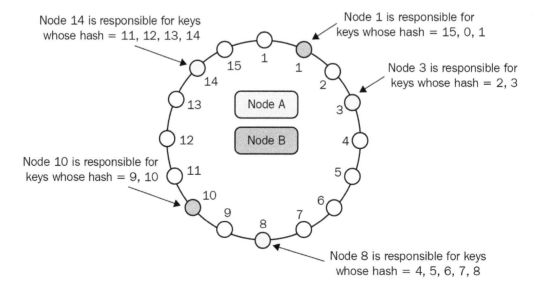

Figure 7.3 – Cassandra replication

As you have probably figured out, Cassandra works very differently from the traditional databases we are used to. It can be complicated to understand and therefore takes some research and experimentation to get comfortable with. However, it can also be very powerful and is widely used by huge companies.

The CAP theorem is a complex topic that entire books could be written about. I have included some further reading at the bottom of this chapter for those who wish to explore it more.

To help us build systems that can achieve all the things we have just discussed, we use various architecture patterns. Let's look at some of them now.

Distributed system patterns

Distributed systems can get complex quickly. Over the years, many patterns have emerged to help us manage and thrive in this complexity. We will explore some of them next.

CQRS

Those who know a little about CQRS might be surprised that one of the first mentions of it in a book about DDD is in the distributed system section. Let's dig into what it is, and then we can revisit this point.

In traditional systems and the monolithic system we built in *Chapter 5, Applying DDD to a Monolithic Application*, we use the same data model and repository to create and read a database from our database. This can work well in a lot of use cases, but as systems develop complexity, it can be hard to manage all the queries and mapping between the data and service layer. Furthermore, systems often have different requirements for reading and writing. For example, a system for capturing analytics might write a lot more than it is read. It could make sense to treat these concerns differently.

Let's take the simple example of a website. When a user views the website, the system might use a query model to get the relevant data to show to the user. If the user does some sort of action to change something (perhaps update their shipping address), the system will issue a command to make this change. A diagram of how the system might look is shown here:

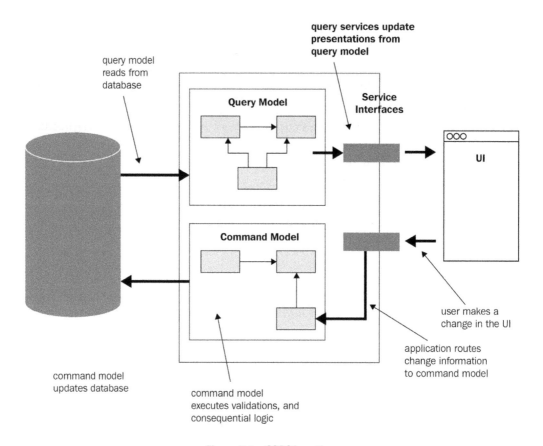

Figure 7.4 – CQRS in action

CQRS is not necessary for DDD, but the sort of complex systems that benefit from DDD may also benefit from exploring CQRS; both are there to help you model and manage complexity.

Bertrand Meyer, the creator of the Eiffel programming language and credited with creating the CQRS pattern, suggests that we follow a few simple rules while implementing CQRS. These are as follows:

- Every method should be a command that performs an action or a query that answers a question. However, no method should do both.

- Asking a question should not change the answer; queries should not mutate.

For **object-oriented (OO)** languages such as Java, these rules are extended to include the following:

- If a method modifies the state of an object, it is a command. It should return void.

- If a method returns a value and its query, it is answering a question. They should not modify the state of an object.

We can adapt these to Golang, as follows:

- If a method modifies the state of the receiver struct or database, it is a command and should return an error or nil

- If a method returns a value, it should not modify the database or its receiver struct

It might be tempting to try to enforce this through an interface, as follows:

```
type Commander interface {
    Command(ctx context.Context, args ...interface{}) error
}
type Querier interface {
    Question(ctx context.Context, args ...interface{})
(interface{}, error)
}
```

But I really do not recommend this. We have lost all benefits of Go's type system here, and our function names give little insight into what the command/query will actually be doing.

So, why is CQRS mentioned in the distributed system section of this book? In monolithic systems, I rarely believe the CQRS pattern is the best option for managing complexity unless implemented perfectly. However, it can work fantastically well for event-based systems (which we talk about a little more next). Commands are a great way to model domain-event emission (for example, writing to Kafka).

EDA

EDA is a pattern in which our distributed system produces, detects, and responds to events. An event is defined as a *significant change in state*. In domain-driven systems, **input and output (I/O)** events travel via a port on a protocol suited to the transport that matches the message bus you are using. For example, RabbitMQ uses the **Advanced Messaging Queuing Protocol (AMQP)** protocol. We will talk about message buses in the message bus section of this chapter.

Events are typically made up of two parts: an event header and an event body. The event header will usually contain some meta-information about the message. For example, it might include a timestamp of when the message was emitted, the system that emitted it, and a **unique identifier (UID)** for that specific message. The body usually contains information about the state that changed. An example body could look like this:

```
{
"event_type": "user.logged_in",
"user_id": 135649039"
}
```

In the preceding example, we have used JSON format, but some other formats popular for defining message schemas are Protobuf, Apache Avro, and Cap'n Proto.

In event-driven systems, there will be a whole variety of messages for varying purposes being emitted. For example, they could be logging, measuring system health, or used for dynamically provisioning resources. The message type we are interested in regarding DDD is **domain events**. For example, we might be interested in a message called user.loggedIn or purchase.failed. These example domain events would be output by one of the microservices in our distributed system and ingested by another.

These domain events might have significance in one specific bounded context but mean nothing to another. This is to be expected and encouraged; there is no expectation that every system is interested in every domain event. If a domain event is interesting within our bounded context, we can transform it into a shape that makes sense for our domain model and take action on it.

Individual domain events might not mean too much by themselves, and it might be they represent only a small part of longer-running tasks. We therefore might need to chain multiple events and systems together to yield the outcome we want. An example is provided here:

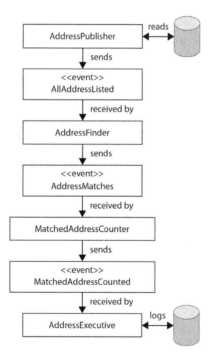

Figure 7.5 – A pipeline of domain events

In this example, you can see how a long-running process starts with us initiating a long-running task that goes through a series of pipeline steps before it becomes useful at the end.

Pipelining such as this is powerful as the system is very flexible. For example, it might be that another system is interested in the `addressesMatched` event and can subscribe from there. It might also be in the future we want to adapt this pipeline to add a new business requirement. For example, maybe we have a requirement that if `addressesMatched` < 500, we trigger a smaller more lightweight process. This would be very easy for us to add.

One major problem event-driven systems face is the distributed nature of the data. For example, if I have a long-running process such as that defined previously, and someone changes their address mid-way through the process, how do we handle that? What if the change they made means we need to cancel our process to ensure the business requirements remain enforced in our system? Let's explore a couple of patterns for dealing with this problem.

Dealing with failure

Earlier in this chapter, we discussed the CAP theorem and the concept of having to choose which compromises in our system to make. Alongside this, we must expect that our distributed system will fail due to both factors outside of our control and edge-case failure modes that we accept can happen from time to time, but we accept that risk in favor of delivery speed. Next, we will discuss some patterns we can put in place to mitigate some of these failures.

Two-phase commit (2PC)

As we discussed earlier, consistency is equally (if not more so) important in a distributed system as it is in a monolithic architecture. However, it is near impossible to create distributed transactions and commit atomically. One approach to solve this is to split our work into two phases:

- **Preparation phase**: We ask each of our sub-systems if it can promise to do the workload we want to complete.
- **Completion phase**: Tell each sub-system to do the work it just promised to do.

In the preparation phase, each of the sub-systems will complete whatever action is necessary to ensure it can keep its promise. In a lot of situations, this is putting a lock around a resource. If any of the participants cannot make this commitment, or if a specified time interval passes without hearing from the coordinator, the workload is aborted.

A diagram of how this looks conceptually is provided here:

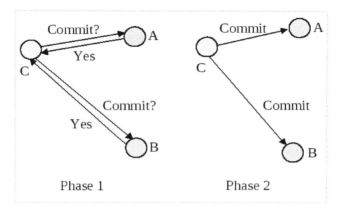

Figure 7.6 – 2PC in action

2PC is a useful pattern to be aware of when building a domain-driven system. Remember—our job as engineers, and especially those who have committed to working in a domain-driven way, is to ensure the system reflects the business domain model as closely as possible. If something goes wrong, the 2PC has a compensating control (the rollback) that helps to ensure that business invariants are not broken. The biggest disadvantage of the 2PC is the fact that it's a blocking protocol. This means in the best case we lose some of the concurrency ability within our system, and in the worst case, no work can be completed at all until the lock is released (either manually or when a pre-specified threshold expires). There are a few other patterns that aim to improve on this, one of which is the saga pattern.

The saga pattern

The saga pattern aims to allow us to achieve consistency within a distributed system without preventing concurrency.

The basic principle of the saga pattern is a simple one; for each action we take within our system, we also define a compensating action that we call in the event we need to roll back.

Let's look at an example. The following diagram shows the flow of an order being created through to customer notification:

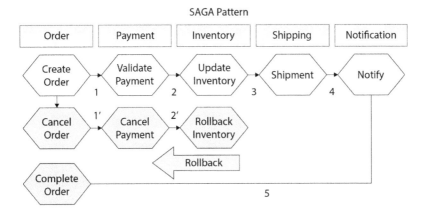

Figure 7.7 – What a saga pattern might look like for an e-commerce system

The blue hexagons represent the happy path. If all goes well, we will simply move from step 1 through to 5 where our order is complete. However, if the system fails at any point, we roll back all the actions before it. Therefore, if the update inventory failed, we would call rollback inventory, cancel payment, and cancel the order. If all these steps successfully resolve or roll back, we should have a consistent system.

The obvious flaw here is this: what if our compensating controls fail too? This is where we can combine the saga pattern with an EDA (that we mentioned previously) and emit an event for compensating control. This means it can be retried by consumer services at their own pace and using their own patterns.

Implementing a resilient saga pattern is challenging and beyond the scope of this book. However, a naïve implementation that can hopefully serve as a useful reference and starting point might look like this:

```go
package chapter7

import "context"

type Saga interface {
    Execute(ctx context.Context) error
    Rollback(ctx context.Context) error
}


type OrderCreator struct{}
func (o OrderCreator) Execute(ctx context.Context) error {
    return o.createOrder(ctx)
}
func (o OrderCreator) Rollback(ctx context.Context) error {
```

```go
        //Rollback Saga here
        return nil
    }
func (o OrderCreator) createOrder(ctx context.Context) error {
    // Create Order here
    return nil
}


type PaymentCreator struct{}
func (p PaymentCreator) Execute(ctx context.Context) error {
    return p.createPayment(ctx)
}
func (p PaymentCreator) Rollback(ctx context.Context) error {
    //Rollback Saga here
    return nil
}
func (p PaymentCreator) createPayment(ctx context.Context)
error {
    // Create payment here
    return nil
}


type SagaManager struct {
    actions []Saga
}
func (s SagaManager) Handle(ctx context.Context) {
    for i, action := range s.actions {
        if err := action.Execute(ctx); err != nil {
            for j := 0; j <= i; j++ {
                if err := s.actions[j].Rollback(ctx); err != nil {
                    // One of our compensation actions failed; we
need to handle it (perhaps by emitting a message to a
                    // a messagebus.
                }
            }
        }
    }
}
```

In the preceding code block, we declare an interface called `Saga`. Anything that has an `Execute` function that returns an error and a `Rollback` function that returns an error satisfies our `Saga` interface. For demonstration purposes, I have declared `OrderCreator` and `PaymentCreator` structs that satisfy this interface. Finally, I create a struct called a `SagaManager` and create a `Handle` function.

In this `Handle` function, I range over all the registered actions. If none of them returns an error, we can assume the saga is complete and our system is in a consistent state. If one of them fails, we call `Rollback` on each of the actions we executed so far. In the simple example, we do not take an action if the rollback fails, but you may want to trigger an alert in this instance to notify an engineer that the system is not in a consistent state, or perhaps emit an event to a message bus that allows you to retry the rollback later.

We have used the term *message bus* a few times so far, so let's review what we mean by that phrase.

What is a message bus?

The term *message bus* originates from enterprise architecture patterns. The pattern aims to:

- Create a common data model and command set shared through a set of shared interfaces
- Allow decoupling of applications so that old ones could be taken away and new ones added with minimal disruption

A shared file could technically satisfy the definition of a message bus (and that is kind of what Kafka is).

In modern software development, we have many different flavors of message buses at our disposal. Purists may argue that some of the tools suggested here aren't technically message buses—they are message queues. The distinction is that the definition of *message bus* does not say anything about guaranteed ordering or other queue-like semantics. Truthfully, I think it's unimportant, and it's more important to ensure you pick the correct tool for what you are trying to achieve. Next, I have included a few popular message bus options and a short summary of why you might or might not use them. I hope this is useful as a jumping-off point for further discovery.

Kafka

Kafka is open sourced by the **Apache Software Foundation** (**ASF**). It was originally created by Linkedin and has become incredibly popular due to its versatility in use. Kafka can be scaled to achieve millions of requests per second and is popular at internet-scale companies such as Microsoft and Cloudflare due to its ability to scale and keep latency low, while also being fault-tolerant.

A typical Kafka architecture looks like this:

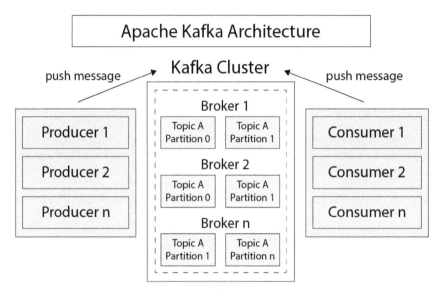

Figure 7.8 – Architecture of Kafka

Firstly, we have a broker. This is responsible for storing messages sent in topics. Topics can be split into many partitions.

Producers are services that connect to Kafka to send messages. They will specify a target a topic and a partition.

Consumers subscribe to topics and partitions to read messages. We can group multiple instances of a consumer together for scalability reasons. They will work together to read all messages from a topic in what is called a consumer group. Services can be both consumers and producers. For example, you might consume from one topic, do some processing, and produce to another.

One challenge of Kafka is that you must know quite a lot about it to use it effectively, and it's easy to make mistakes that can have dire consequences for your application (for example, you can very easily cause messages to be delivered out of order if you use the wrong partitioning strategy). Furthermore, monitoring it can be difficult, and running your own cluster is not for the faint of heart.

RabbitMQ

RabbitMQ is also an open source queuing system based on the AMQP protocol. It is easy to get started with and conceptually is simple. Messages are sent by producers to an exchange, which forwards them to one or many queues. Once a message has been read from a queue and acknowledged by a producer application, it is consumed and will never be received again. RabbitMQ comes packaged with a nice UI that gives you some visibility into what is happening.

Here's an example overview of the **Admin** dashboard:

Figure 7.9 – RabbitMQ Admin dashboard

RabbitMQ's architecture shares some similarities with Kafka's:

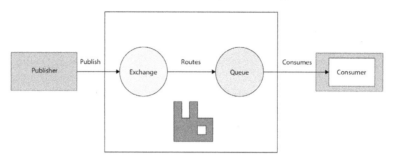

Figure 7.10 – Architecture of RabbitMQ

The publisher sends messages to an exchange. Based on the routing key, it is sent to a specific queue where is it picked up by a consumer application to process.

The disadvantages of RabbitMQ are mostly that it doesn't scale quite as well or as easily as Kafka. It also only offers a subset of the features that Kafka does. In my experience, as companies scale both in terms of workloads and teams, they start to want a richer feature set and usually start exploring migrating to Kafka.

NATS

Neural Autonomic Transport System (**NATS**) is an open source streaming system written in Golang. This makes it a great option for learning more about how some of these technologies work under the hood as the code is very readable.

NATS has some similarities with Kafka, in that you publish messages to subjects, and they are consumed by subscribers. One nice feature of NATS is the ability to wildcard match on topics such as those shown here:

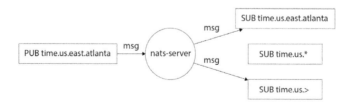

Figure 7.11 – Architecture of NATS

The biggest thing you need to consider when using NATS is its durability. NATS guarantees at-most-once delivery, which is to say your message might never be delivered at all. However, in return for this, you get an incredibly simple-to-run streaming system. Due to how lightweight it is and its speed, it is commonly used for IoT use cases.

Summary

The goal of this chapter was to highlight that DDD is not the entire story, and there are patterns and tools out there that can help you navigate the complexity you may experience as you work on bigger systems. We barely scratched the surface of most of these topics, so I have included further reading next that will hopefully help you explore some of these topics deeper if they interest you.

Further reading

- CAP theorem: `https://en.wikipedia.org/wiki/CAP_theorem`

- Using Kafka at scale: `https://blog.cloudflare.com/using-apache-kafka-to-process-1-trillion-messages/`

- Getting started with RabbitMQ: `https://www.cloudamqp.com/blog/part1-rabbitmq-for-beginners-what-is-rabbitmq.html`

- NATS overview: `https://docs.nats.io/nats-concepts/overview`

8

TDD, BDD, and DDD

We have now covered all the core concepts of **domain-driven design** (**DDD**). However, you will often see the suite of acronyms that make up this chapter's title in the same sentence, especially on job postings and résumés. What do they mean? Are they related to DDD?

In this chapter, we will do the following:

- Discuss and give examples of TDD and BDD using Go

- Talk about how TDD and BDD can be used alongside DDD to make your systems more resilient and maintainable

Technical requirements

In this chapter, we will write a large amount of Golang code. To be able to follow along, you will need the following:

- Golang installed on your machine. You can find instructions to install it here: `https://go.dev/doc/install`. The following code was written with Go 1.19.3 installed, so anything later than this should be fine.

- Some sort of text editor or IDE. Some popular options are Visual Studio Code (`https://code.visualstudio.com/download`) or GoLand (`https://www.jetbrains.com/help/go/installation-guide.html`). All screenshots in this section are taken from GoLand.

- Access to GitHub. All code for this section can be found here: `https://github.com/PacktPublishing/Domain-Driven-Design-with-GoLang/tree/main/chapter8`.

TDD

TDD stands for **test-driven development**. It is a process in which you write tests for business requirements before your software is fully developed. As you write code, you repeatedly update your test cases until you are satisfied the code satisfies the business requirements. The goal is to write "just enough" code to pass the tests and no more. A diagram representing this process is shown here:

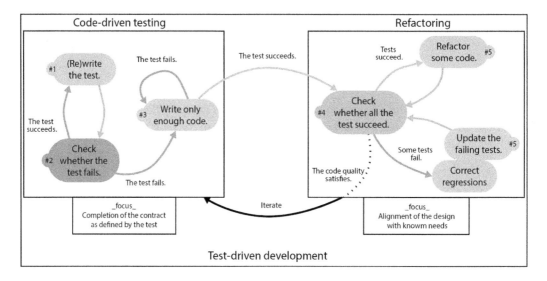

Figure 8.1 – TDD flow chart

Let's look at each of the steps in isolation. If we were developing a new feature for our application, we would do the following:

1. **Add a test**: Before we write any code, we write the test case. You might write this in the form of a user story such as *"As an API user, I want to be able to see a user's balance across all their accounts when I call the /balances endpoint so that I can display it on the home screen,"* or by using the *Given-When-Then* method: *"Given I am an API user, when I call /balances, I get a user's balances across all accounts."*

    As you can see, we have not written a single line of code yet, and we are focusing deeply on the business requirements. This should hopefully highlight immediately why TDD and DDD are complementary patterns.

2. **Run the test we just wrote. It should fail (and we should expect it to)**: This proves that the expected behavior isn't already available in our code, that our testing framework is set up correctly, and rules out the possibility that we wrote a flawed test that is always going to pass.

3. **Write as little code as possible to pass the test**: This is not the time to write elegant code. At this stage, spaghetti code or confusing, inefficient code is welcome. The goal is to get that test case passing by any means necessary while solving for the business invariant.

4. **Rerun the tests – the new one and all the previous ones should now pass**: This validates that the code we have written not only solves the new behavior but also didn't break existing behavior.

5. **Refactor**: Now that we have added our new feature, it's time to revisit the spaghetti code we wrote to pass the test and make it beautiful and ready for code review. With each change we make, we can rerun the test suite to ensure our refactor did not change behavior.

That's all there is to TDD. It can also be used to debug or improve legacy code. For example, you could write tests to give yourself confidence that the code works as you expect and then refactor it to ensure the tests still pass.

Now that we understand TDD in principle, let's imagine we were given this ticket to complete:

Title: As a customer, when I purchase a cookie, I get an email receipt.

Description: Customers like to purchase cookies. They also like to claim them as a business expense. We need to add support for purchasing a cookie and sending an email receipt to a customer.

This is the acceptance criteria:

*   *Given that a user tries to purchase a cookie and we have them in stock when they tap their card, they get charged and then receive an email receipt a few moments later*

*   *Given that a user tries to purchase a cookie and we don't have any in stock, we return an error to the cashier so they can apologize to the customer*

*   *Given that a user tries to purchase a cookie and we have them in stock, but their card gets declined, we return an error to the cashier so that we can ban the customer from the store*

*   *Given that a user purchases a cookie and we have them in stock, their card is charged successfully, but we fail to send an email, we return a message to the cashier so they can notify the customer that they will not get an email, but the transaction is still considered complete*

This ticket describes the expected user behaviors for us. Let's look at how we might follow TDD step by step to complete this task in Go.

Adding a test

Let's make a new file called `cookies_test.go`, as well as `cookies.go`. Your directory should now look as follows:

Figure 8.2 – Our directory structure after making our new files

Note how my IDE has detected that `cookies_test.go` is a test file and has highlighted it in green. This is because, in Go, any file with `_test.go` is a test file. This means they will be ignored when you compile your binary. Tests are first-class citizens in Go and TDD is very easy to implement, as you will see!

In `cookies_test.go`, let's add the following lines:

```
package chapter8_test


import "testing"


func Test_CookiePurchases(t *testing.T) {
    t.Run(`Given a user tries to purchase a cookie and we have
them in stock,
        "when they tap their card, they get charged and then
receive an email receipt a few moments later.`,
        func(t *testing.T) {})
}
```

Firstly, you can see we have declared our package as `chapter8_test`. This is different from `cookies.go`, which will be declared as in the `chapter8` package. The reason I recommend doing this is it ensures you test your code as a consumer. This is called black-box testing. Testing this way makes your tests less brittle because you are not depending on specific implementation details, as they should be private and we will not be able to access them.

Next, we declare a test function. In Go, `Test` functions start with `Test_` and then usually the name of the function we are testing. We haven't made a function yet, so for now, I have called it `CookiePurchases`. We might update this later. You'll see that our function takes a parameter of type `*testing.T`. This helps Go to identify your test functions and gives us some really helpful testing utilities, which we will see shortly.

Next, we create a closure function using t.Run. This allows you to create sub-tests within a test function and is simply used for grouping related tests. This is not necessary, and you'll see a lot of code that does not follow this approach. However, I really like it.

Note that I have named my test exactly what was in the acceptance criteria of our ticket. This is where TDD really shows that it is a complementary approach to DDD. The latter is all about ensuring our system is modeling a real-world domain. Ideally, our acceptance criteria should have come from a domain expert. By writing tests like this, we are ensuring our code does match real-world expectations, and it also serves as fantastic documentation for the next developer who comes along and works on our code.

Before we move on to *step 2*, we will add one more line to our test:

```
func Test_CookiePurchases(t *testing.T) {
    t.Run(`Given a user tries to purchase a cookie and we have
them in stock,
        "when they tap their card, they get charged and then
receive an email receipt a few moments later.`,
        func(t *testing.T) {
            t.FailNow()
        })
}
```

We have added t.FailNow(). Why did we do this? In Go, if a test is empty, it passes immediately. This means we will break our rule that says, "The test should fail." It also signifies both to our future selves and any other engineers who may work on the code base that this test is incomplete, and we intend to implement it. If you had thousands of tests in your code base and you left this one empty and passing, it could get overlooked, and you could end up with a gap in your testing. Finally, it proves that when we run it in a moment, the Go test harness is set up correctly.

Run the test we just wrote – it should fail (and we should expect it to)

Let's run our test. In GoLand, I do this by clicking the gutter icon, as seen here. However, you can also run tests from the command line by running go test ./....

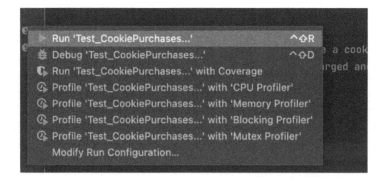

Figure 8.3 – Running a test in GoLand by clicking on the left-hand gutter

You will see output such as the following:

```
=== RUN    Test_CookiePurchases
=== RUN    Test_CookiePurchases/Given_a_user_tries_to_
purchase_a_cookie_and_we_have_them_in_stock,____"when_they_
tap_their_card,_they_get_charged_and_then_receive_an_email_
receipt_a_few_moments_later.
--- FAIL: Test_CookiePurchases (0.00s)
    --- FAIL: Test_CookiePurchases/Given_a_user_tries_to_
purchase_a_cookie_and_we_have_them_in_stock,____"when_they_
tap_their_card,_they_get_charged_and_then_receive_an_email_
receipt_a_few_moments_later. (0.00s)


FAIL


Process finished with the exit code 1
```

Great, our test is failing! Let's move on to *step 3*.

Write as little code as possible to pass the test

We currently have not written any code at all. In `cookies.go`, let's write the minimum code possible that satisfies the test criteria. The following is my attempt, but as an exercise, please attempt it yourself. Remember that the goal here isn't beautiful code; it's to get the test passing.

Here is what I wrote:

```go
package chapter8

import "context"

type (
    EmailSender interface {
        SendEmailReceipt(ctx context.Context, emailAddress string) error
    }
    CardCharger interface {
        ChargeCard(ctx context.Context, cardToken string, amountInCents int) error
    }
    CookieStockChecker interface {
        AmountInStock(ctx context.Context) int
    }

    CookieService struct {
        emailSender  EmailSender
        cardCharger  CardCharger
        stockChecker CookieStockChecker
    }
)

func NewCookieService(e EmailSender, c CardCharger, a CookieStockChecker) (*CookieService, error) {
    return &CookieService{
        emailSender:  e,
        cardCharger:  c,
        stockChecker: a,
    }, nil
}

func (c *CookieService) PurchaseCookies(ctx context.Context, amountOfCookiesToPurchase int) error {
    //TODO: ask how much cookies cost. This is a placeholder.
    priceOfCookie := 5
```

```
cookiesInStock := c.stockChecker.AmountInStock(ctx)
if amountOfCookiesToPurchase > cookiesInStock {
    //TODO: what do I do in this situation?
}
cost := priceOfCookie * amountOfCookiesToPurchase

//TODO: where do I get cardtoken from?
if err := c.cardCharger.ChargeCard(ctx, "some-token", cost);
err != nil {
    //TODO: handle this later.
}

if err := c.emailSender.SendEmailReceipt(ctx, "some-email");
err != nil {
    //TODO: handle error later
}
return nil
}
```

Note that as I wrote the code, I put lots of TODO comments and left notes to myself to either implement functionality later or to check with our domain expert about how they see a specific situation being handled. We will revisit that shortly, but for now, we are not concerned; let's get our test passing.

In my implementation, I defined some interfaces. We need some mocks of these interfaces to be able to test our code. By mocking interfaces, it allows us to easily create situations in our code that might be otherwise hard to achieve. For example, if we want to test a specific fork in our code when an email doesn't send, we can do that very easily and do not need to depend on setting up a buggy email infrastructure. Furthermore, interfaces ensure that our code is decoupled from specific implementations. For example, if we were using Google as our email provider and switched to AWS, we would only need to change the adaptor package. (We covered the adaptor pattern earlier in this book.)

The Go team provides a mocking framework called gomock. You can read more about it here: https://github.com/golang/mock. gomock allows you to generate all the code you need to mock an interface. Let's generate mocks for ours now. To do this, we create gen.go at the root of our project and add the following:

```
package gen

import _ "github.com/golang/mock/mockgen/model"
```

```
//go:generate mockgen -package mocks -destination
chapter8/mocks/cookies.go github.com/PacktPublishing/
Domain-Driven-Design-with-GoLang/chapter8
CookieStockChecker,CardCharger,EmailSender
```

You can find more instructions on how this works in the gomock README file. Your gen.go file might look a little different, depending on how you solved the task. Furthermore, if you want to write manual mocks, then that is fine too.

To generate the mocks, we run go generate ./....

If all goes well, we should now see a new directory, as follows:

Figure 8.4 – After generation, the mocks folder should be created

Let's now update our test:

```
func Test_CookiePurchases(t *testing.T) {
    t.Run(`Given a user tries to purchase a cookie and we have
them in stock,
        "when they tap their card, they get charged and then
receive an email receipt a few moments later.`,
        func(t *testing.T) {
            var (
                ctrl = gomock.NewController(t)
                e    = mocks.NewMockEmailSender(ctrl)
                c    = mocks.NewMockCardCharger(ctrl)
                s    = mocks.NewMockCookieStockChecker(ctrl)

                ctx = context.Background()
            )
            cookiesToBuy := 5
            totalExpectedCost := 25

            cs, err := chapter8.NewCookieService(e, c, s)
            if err != nil {
```

```
            t.Fatalf("expected no error but got %v", err)
        }

        gomock.InOrder(
            s.EXPECT().AmountInStock(ctx).Times(1).
Return(cookiesToBuy),
            c.EXPECT().ChargeCard(ctx, "some-token",
totalExpectedCost).Times(1).Return(nil),
            e.EXPECT().SendEmailReceipt(ctx, "some-email").
Times(1).Return(nil),
        )

        err = cs.PurchaseCookies(ctx, cookiesToBuy)
        if err != nil {
            t.Fatalf("expected no error but got %v", err)
        }
    })
}
```

In the preceding snippet, we have created instances of the mocks we generated. These mocks satisfy the interfaces we need, so we can call `NewCookieService`. We then use a utility function of `gomock`, which allows us to ensure that the interface functions are called only once and with the exact parameters we expect. Finally, we call `PurchaseCookies` and make sure we get no error.

This test passes and satisfies the criteria outlined in the test description, but we left lots of TODO comments for things we need to clarify with our domain experts. The following outlines the questions I had and the answers the domain expert gave.

Q: How much do cookies cost? Does it ever change?

A: Cookies cost 50 cents. That could change in the future, but for now, they will be that much.

Q: In the event that someone wants to purchase more cookies than we have in stock, what should we do?

A: We should give them the ones we have in stock.

Q: How do we find a user's card token? Does another team provide this, or do we need to build this functionality?

A: When a customer presents their card, our card machine automatically gives us the token. Therefore, we should have access to the card token.

Q: How do we find a user's email address?

A: We receive it from the machine automatically, like we do the card token.

Great! We now have learned more about how our system should operate. We should ensure we have test cases that cover these scenarios too. Let's write them now while we remember.

Our test file now has the following test stubs in it (in addition to the one we filled in):

```
t.Run(`Given a user tries to purchase a cookie and we don't
have any in stock, we return an error to the cashier
      so they can apologize to the customer.`, func(t
*testing.T) {
})


t.Run(`Given a user tries to purchase a cookie, we have them in
stock, but their card gets declined, we return
    an error to the cashier so that we can ban the customer from
the store.`, func(t *testing.T) {


})
t.Run(`Given a user purchases a cookie and we have them in
stock, their card is charged successfully but we
    fail to send an email, we return a message to the cashier so
they know can notify the customer that they will not
    get an e-mail, but the transaction is still considered
done.`, func(t *testing.T) {


})


t.Run(`Given someone wants to purchase more cookies than we
have in stock we only charge them for the ones we do have`,
    func(t *testing.T) {


})
```

We can now move on to the final TDD step.

Refactoring

We can now refactor our code to make it neater. The only change I will make at this point is to change cookiePrice to 50. This should make our test fail.

After changing cookiePrice to 50, I then run the test again:

```
--- FAIL: Test_CookiePurchases (0.00s)
=== RUN    Test_CookiePurchases/Given_a_user_tries_to_
purchase_a_cookie_and_we_have_them_in_stock,____"when_they_
tap_their_card,_they_get_charged_and_then_receive_an_email_
receipt_a_few_moments_later.
    cookies.go:42: Unexpected call to *mocks.MockCardCharger.
ChargeCard([context.Background some-token 250]) at /Users/
matthewboyle/Dev/ddd-golang/chapter8/cookies.go:42 because:
        expected call at /Users/matthewboyle/Dev/ddd-golang/
chapter8/cookies_test.go:35 doesn't match the argument at index
2.
        Got: 250 (int)
        Want: is equal to 25 (int)
```

This is what we expected. Let's update our test to correct the expected totalPrice:

```
t.Run(`Given a user tries to purchase a cookie and we have them
in stock,
    "when they tap their card, they get charged and then receive
an email receipt a few moments later.`,
    func(t *testing.T) {
        var (
            ctrl = gomock.NewController(t)
            e    = mocks.NewMockEmailSender(ctrl)
            c    = mocks.NewMockCardCharger(ctrl)
            s    = mocks.NewMockCookieStockChecker(ctrl)

            ctx = context.Background()
        )
        cookiesToBuy := 5
        totalExpectedCost := 250

        cs, err := chapter8.NewCookieService(e, c, s)
        if err != nil {
```

```
            t.Fatalf("expected no error but got %v", err)
        }


        gomock.InOrder(
            s.EXPECT().AmountInStock(ctx).Times(1).
Return(cookiesToBuy),
            c.EXPECT().ChargeCard(ctx, "some-token",
totalExpectedCost).Times(1).Return(nil),
            e.EXPECT().SendEmailReceipt(ctx, "some-email").
Times(1).Return(nil),
        )


        err = cs.PurchaseCookies(ctx, cookiesToBuy)
        if err != nil {
            t.Fatalf("expected no error but got %v", err)
        }
    })
```

We run the test again and it passes.

Let's fill in the other tests. Have a go at doing it yourself, and we will walk through the approach as follows:

```
t.Run(`Given a user tries to purchase a cookie and we don't
have any in stock, we return an error to the cashier
        so they can apologize to the customer.`, func(t
*testing.T) {
    var (
        ctrl = gomock.NewController(t)
        e    = mocks.NewMockEmailSender(ctrl)
        c    = mocks.NewMockCardCharger(ctrl)
        s    = mocks.NewMockCookieStockChecker(ctrl)


        ctx = context.Background()
    )
    cookiesToBuy := 5


    cs, err := chapter8.NewCookieService(e, c, s)
    if err != nil {
        t.Fatalf("expected no error but got %v", err)
```

```
    }

    gomock.InOrder(
        s.EXPECT().AmountInStock(ctx).Times(1).Return(0),
    )

    err = cs.PurchaseCookies(ctx, cookiesToBuy)
    if err == nil {
        t.Fatal("expected an error but got none")
    }
})
```

This test fails when we run it, as it does not return early with an error, even though we return no cookies in stock. Let's write some code to ensure this test case passes.

I have added the following code:

```
func (c *CookieService) PurchaseCookies(ctx context.Context,
amountOfCookiesToPurchase int) error {
    priceOfCookie := 50

    cookiesInStock := c.stockChecker.AmountInStock(ctx)
    if cookiesInStock == 0 {
        return errors.New("no cookies in stock sorry :(")
    }
    if amountOfCookiesToPurchase > cookiesInStock {
        //TODO: what do I do in this situation?
    }
    ...
```

If we run the test again, it now passes. We should also run the last test to ensure that it still passes too. It does? Great!

Let's fill in the next test:

```
t.Run(`Given a user tries to purchase a cookie, we have them in
stock, but their card gets declined, we return
    an error to the cashier so that we can ban the customer from
the store.`, func(t *testing.T) {
    var (
```

```
        ctrl = gomock.NewController(t)
        e    = mocks.NewMockEmailSender(ctrl)
        c    = mocks.NewMockCardCharger(ctrl)
        s    = mocks.NewMockCookieStockChecker(ctrl)

        ctx = context.Background()
    )
    cookiesToBuy := 5
    totalExpectedCost := 250

    cs, err := chapter8.NewCookieService(e, c, s)
    if err != nil {
        t.Fatalf("expected no error but got %v", err)
    }

    gomock.InOrder(
        s.EXPECT().AmountInStock(ctx).Times(1).
Return(cookiesToBuy),
        c.EXPECT().ChargeCard(ctx, "some-token",
totalExpectedCost).Times(1).Return(errors.New("some error")),
    )

    err = cs.PurchaseCookies(ctx, cookiesToBuy)
    if err == nil {
        t.Fatal("expected an error but got none")
    }
    if err.Error() != "your card was declined, you are banned!"
{
        t.Fatalf("error was unexpected, got %v", err.Error())
    }
})
```

In this test, we are asserting that the call to charge the card fails and we get back a specific error text. Let's run the test.

It fails as expected with the following error:

```
=== RUN    Test_CookiePurchases
--- FAIL: Test_CookiePurchases (0.00s)
=== RUN    Test_CookiePurchases/Given_a_user_tries_to_
purchase_a_cookie,_we_have_them_in_stock,_but_their_card_gets_
declined,_we_return____an_error_to_the_cashier_so_that_we_can_
ban_the_customer_from_the_store.
    cookies.go:51: Unexpected call to *mocks.MockEmailSender.
SendEmailReceipt([context.Background some-email]) at /Users/
matthewboyle/Dev/ddd-golang/chapter8/cookies.go:51 because:
there are no expected calls of the method "SendEmailReceipt"
for that receiver
```

This is because an error is never returned when we fail to charge the card. Let's write the minimal amount of code to fix this:

```
...
if amountOfCookiesToPurchase > cookiesInStock {
    //TODO: what do I do in this situation?
}
cost := priceOfCookie * amountOfCookiesToPurchase

//TODO: where do I get cardtoken from?
if err := c.cardCharger.ChargeCard(ctx, "some-token", cost);
err != nil {
    return errors.New("your card was declined, you are banned!")
}
...
```

Let's run our test again:

```
=== RUN    Test_CookiePurchases
--- PASS: Test_CookiePurchases (0.00s)
=== RUN    Test_CookiePurchases/Given_a_user_tries_to_
purchase_a_cookie,_we_have_them_in_stock,_but_their_card_gets_
declined,_we_return____an_error_to_the_cashier_so_that_we_can_
ban_the_customer_from_the_store.
    --- PASS: Test_CookiePurchases/Given_a_user_tries_to_
purchase_a_cookie,_we_have_them_in_stock,_but_their_card_gets_
declined,_we_return____an_error_to_the_cashier_so_that_we_can_
```

```
ban_the_customer_from_the_store. (0.00s)
PASS
```

Great! It now passes, and our other tests do too. Now is the time to do some refactoring if you want to. I am happy enough with the code for now, so I'm going to move on to the next test:

```
t.Run(`Given a user purchases a cookie and we have them in
stock, their card is charged successfully but we
    fail to send an email, we return a message to the cashier so
they know can notify the customer that they will not
    get an e-mail, but the transaction is still considered
done.`, func(t *testing.T) {
    var (
        ctrl = gomock.NewController(t)
        e    = mocks.NewMockEmailSender(ctrl)
        c    = mocks.NewMockCardCharger(ctrl)
        s    = mocks.NewMockCookieStockChecker(ctrl)

        ctx = context.Background()
    )
    cookiesToBuy := 5
    totalExpectedCost := 250

    cs, err := chapter8.NewCookieService(e, c, s)
    if err != nil {
        t.Fatalf("expected no error but got %v", err)
    }

    gomock.InOrder(
        s.EXPECT().AmountInStock(ctx).Times(1).
Return(cookiesToBuy),
        c.EXPECT().ChargeCard(ctx, "some-token",
totalExpectedCost).Times(1).Return(nil),
        e.EXPECT().SendEmailReceipt(ctx, "some-email").Times(1).
Return(errors.New("failed to send email")),
    )

    err = cs.PurchaseCookies(ctx, cookiesToBuy)
```

```
    if err == nil {
        t.Fatal("expected an error but got none")
    }
    if err.Error() != "we are sorry but the email receipt did
not send" {
        t.Fatalf("error was unexpected, got %v", err.Error())
    }
})
```

Hopefully, this test is clear to you at this point. We are again asserting that certain calls happen but that our email fails to send, and we get a particular error text back.

Brief aside: at this point, I am certain some of you are screaming at me, *"Why do you keep repeating the same boilerplate code for setting up a test?! Doesn't that break the don't repeat yourself (DRY) principle?!"* You are, of course, correct; however, this is a pattern I have landed on after many years of trying to make tests as succinct as code. I find that tests such as the preceding ones are the best documentation we can have, and ensuring that every test has all the information you need to figure out what it is doing outlined clearly is the best way to ensure other engineers (and your future self) can get up to speed with the code base. It's also the reason I am not a big proponent of table-driven tests, which are popular in the Go community; I feel they prioritize speed for the writer of the code rather than for the future reader. Code is written once but read many times, so we should always prioritize the reader.

Back to our code. We simply add this line:

```
if err := c.emailSender.SendEmailReceipt(ctx, "some-email");
err != nil {
    return errors.New("we are sorry but the email receipt did
not send")
}
```

This test now passes too.

Let's move promptly on to the next test. The next one is a little bit more interesting:

```
t.Run(`Given someone wants to purchase more cookies than we
have in stock we only charge them for the ones we do have`,
    func(t *testing.T) {
        var (
            ctrl = gomock.NewController(t)
            e    = mocks.NewMockEmailSender(ctrl)
            c    = mocks.NewMockCardCharger(ctrl)
            s    = mocks.NewMockCookieStockChecker(ctrl)
```

```
            ctx = context.Background()
        )
        requestedCookiesToBuy := 5
        inStock := 3
        totalExpectedCost := 150

        cs, err := chapter8.NewCookieService(e, c, s)
        if err != nil {
            t.Fatalf("expected no error but got %v", err)
        }

        gomock.InOrder(
            s.EXPECT().AmountInStock(ctx).Times(1).
Return(inStock),
            c.EXPECT().ChargeCard(ctx, "some-token",
totalExpectedCost).Times(1).Return(nil),
            e.EXPECT().SendEmailReceipt(ctx, "some-email").
Times(1).Return(nil),
        )

        err = cs.PurchaseCookies(ctx, requestedCookiesToBuy)
        if err != nil {
            t.Fatalf("expected no error but got %v", err)
        }
    })
```

In this test, we are requesting a different number of cookies than are available. As per the domain expert's requirements, we need to only charge for the ones we have in stock and follow the regular flow apart from that.

This test fails right now, as we are not handling this case:

```
=== RUN    Test_CookiePurchases
--- FAIL: Test_CookiePurchases (0.00s)
=== RUN    Test_CookiePurchases/Given_someone_wants_to_purchase_
more_cookies_than_we_have_in_stock_we_only_charge_them_for_the_
ones_we_do_have
    cookies.go:47: Unexpected call to *mocks.MockCardCharger.
ChargeCard([context.Background some-token 250]) at /Users/
matthewboyle/Dev/ddd-golang/chapter8/cookies.go:47 because:
```

```
        expected call at /Users/matthewboyle/Dev/ddd-golang/
chapter8/cookies_test.go:159 doesn't match the argument at
index 2.
        Got: 250 (int)
        Want: is equal to 150 (int)
```

Right now, we are charging for cookies we do not have in stock. Let's fix this:

```
func (c *CookieService) PurchaseCookies(ctx context.Context,
amountOfCookiesToPurchase int) error {
    priceOfCookie := 50

    cookiesInStock := c.stockChecker.AmountInStock(ctx)
    if cookiesInStock == 0 {
        return errors.New("no cookies in stock sorry :(")
    }
    if amountOfCookiesToPurchase > cookiesInStock {
        amountOfCookiesToPurchase = cookiesInStock
    }
    cost := priceOfCookie * amountOfCookiesToPurchase
...
```

All we have done here is update amountOfCookiesToPurchase = cookiesInStock in the situation where our request is greater. The test now passes!

If we run go test with code coverage now (go test ./... -cover), we will see we have 100% coverage:

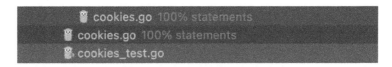

Figure 8.5 – 100% test coverage!

This puts us in a great spot to maintain this code going forward, which is ideal, as we are not quite done yet. We have two requirements we have not implemented yet:

- The domain expert told us we can expect to receive the card token as part of the request

- The domain expert told us we can receive the email as part of the request

Let's update our function signature to add both:

```
func (c *CookieService) PurchaseCookies(
    ctx context.Context,
    amountOfCookiesToPurchase int,
    cardToken string,
    email string,
) error {
```

This has broken all our tests, as we are now not passing the correct parameter. To fix this, let's just quickly add any old string to them, such as the following:

```
...
err = cs.PurchaseCookies(ctx, cookiesToBuy, "a-token", "an-email")
if err != nil {
    t.Fatalf("expected no error but got %v", err)
}
...
```

If we run our tests, they now all fail. This is because we hardcoded placeholder values for these. Let's update our code to make our final version of the function:

```
func (c *CookieService) PurchaseCookies(
    ctx context.Context,
    amountOfCookiesToPurchase int,
    cardToken string,
    email string,
) error {
    priceOfCookie := 50

    cookiesInStock := c.stockChecker.AmountInStock(ctx)
    if cookiesInStock == 0 {
        return errors.New("no cookies in stock sorry :(")
    }
    if amountOfCookiesToPurchase > cookiesInStock {
        amountOfCookiesToPurchase = cookiesInStock
    }
```

```
    cost := priceOfCookie * amountOfCookiesToPurchase

    if err := c.cardCharger.ChargeCard(ctx, cardToken, cost);
err != nil {
        return errors.New("your card was declined, you are
banned!")
    }

    if err := c.emailSender.SendEmailReceipt(ctx, email); err !=
nil {
        return errors.New("we are sorry but the email receipt did
not send")
    }
    return nil
}
```

Here's an example of the changes we need to make to each test:

```
t.Run(`Given a user tries to purchase a cookie and we have them
in stock,
    "when they tap their card, they get charged and then receive
an email receipt a few moments later.`,
    func(t *testing.T) {
        var (
            ctrl = gomock.NewController(t)
            e    = mocks.NewMockEmailSender(ctrl)
            c    = mocks.NewMockCardCharger(ctrl)
            s    = mocks.NewMockCookieStockChecker(ctrl)

            ctx       = context.Background()
            email     = "some@email.com"
            cardToken = "token"
        )
        cookiesToBuy := 5
        totalExpectedCost := 250

        cs, err := chapter8.NewCookieService(e, c, s)
        if err != nil {
```

```
        t.Fatalf("expected no error but got %v", err)
    }

    gomock.InOrder(
        s.EXPECT().AmountInStock(ctx).Times(1).
Return(cookiesToBuy),
        c.EXPECT().ChargeCard(ctx, cardToken,
totalExpectedCost).Times(1).Return(nil),
        e.EXPECT().SendEmailReceipt(ctx, email).Times(1).
Return(nil),
    )

    err = cs.PurchaseCookies(ctx, cookiesToBuy, cardToken,
email)
    if err != nil {
        t.Fatalf("expected no error but got %v", err)
    }
})
```

In the preceding snippet, we have ensured that our mocks get called with the values passed into the function.

You are now a TDD expert! Hopefully, the value of this iterative approach is clear to you, and you can see how you can work with your domain experts to ensure you are iteratively testing and adding the behavior of your domain. If you want to practice a little more, consider adding these requirements to our code:

- The card token cannot be empty and must be 12 characters long. In the event it's empty, we should return an error.

- The e-mail address must be a valid email, it cannot be empty, and we only support @gmail.com, @yahoo.com, and @msn.co.uk domains. We should return an error if this is not true.

- If today's date is January 14, all purchases are free, as it's our store's birthday.

You may want to refactor the code a little bit and break some of this logic out into new functions. However, you can do that in the "refactor step" after successfully implementing the functionality.

Now that we understand TDD and how we can use it alongside DDD, let's look at **behaviour-driven development (BDD)**.

BDD

BDD is an extension of TDD that aims to enable deeper collaboration between engineers, domain experts, and quality assurance engineers (if your company employs them). A diagram of how this works with TDD is shown here.

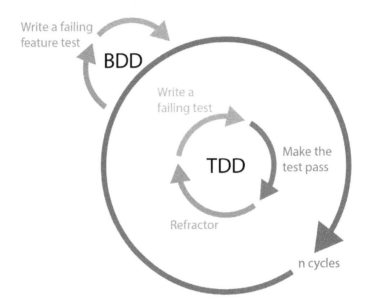

Figure 8.6 – BDD as an extension of TDD

The goal of BDD is to provide a higher level of abstraction from code through a domain-specific language (often referred to as a DSL) that can become executable tests. Two popular frameworks for writing BDD tests is the use of Gherkin (https://cucumber.io/docs/gherkin/reference/) and Cucumber (https://cucumber.io)

Gherkin defines a set of keywords and a language specification. Cucumber reads this text and validates that the software works as expected. For example, the following is a valid Cucumber test:

```
Feature: checkout Integration
Scenario: Successfully Capture a payment
Given I am a customer
When I purchase a cookie for 50 cents.
Then my card should be charged 50 cents and an e-mail receipt
is sent.
```

Some teams work with their domain experts to ensure their acceptance criteria in their ticketing system are in this format. If it is, this criterion can simply become the test. This aligns nicely with DDD.

Now that we have a high-level understanding of BDD, let's take a look at implementing a test in Go. We are going to use the `go-bdd` framework, which you can find at `https://github.com/go-bdd/gobdd`.

Firstly, let's install go-bdd in our project:

```
go get github.com/go-bdd/gobdd
```

Now, create a `features` folder:

Figure 8.7 – Our features folder after creation

Inside the `features` folder, let's add a file called `add.feature` with this inside it:

```
Feature: Adding numbers
  Scenario: add two numbers together
    When I add 3 and 6
    Then the result should equal 9
```

Next, let's add an `add_test.go` file and the following:

```go
package chapter8

import (
    "testing"

    "github.com/go-bdd/gobdd"
)

func add(t gobdd.StepTest, ctx gobdd.Context, first, second int) {
    res := first + second
    ctx.Set("result", res)
}

func check(t gobdd.StepTest, ctx gobdd.Context, sum int) {
    received, err := ctx.GetInt("result")
```

```
    if err != nil {
        t.Fatal(err)
        return
    }
    if sum != received {
        t.Fatalf("expected %d but got %d", sum, received)
    }
}


func TestScenarios(t *testing.T) {
    suite := gobdd.NewSuite(t)
    suite.AddStep(`I add (\d+) and (\d+)`, add)
    suite.AddStep(`the result should equal (\d+)`, check)
    suite.Run()
}
```

In the preceding code, we add a bdd step function called add. This function name is important; the framework knows that when I add 3 and 6 gets mapped to this function. If you change the name of this function to "sum", you'd need to update the feature file to say, when I sum 3 and 6 together. We then perform our logic and store it in the context so that we can recall it later.

We then define a check function that is our actual test; it validates our assertions. Finally, we set up a test suite to run our code.

If you run the preceding test, it should pass.

This might be your first time seeing a BDD-style test, but I bet it's not your first time seeing a unit test. Why is that?

As you can see, although BDD tests are closer to natural language, it pushes a lot of the complexity down into the tests. The preceding example we used is trivial, but if you want to express complex scenarios (such as the cookie example we used previously) there is a lot of scaffolding the developer needs to implement to make the tests work correctly. This can be worthwhile if you have lots of access to your domain experts and you are truly going to work side by side. However, if they are absent or not invested in the process, unit tests are much faster and more engaging for engineering teams to work with. Much like DDD, BDD is a multidisciplinary team investment, and it is worth ensuring you have buy-in from all stakeholders before investing too much time in it.

Summary

In this chapter, we have discussed TDD and BDD and explained how even though they are not necessarily part of the DDD framework, they are certainly complementary patterns that are worth knowing. Even on projects where you do not opt to follow DDD, it is worth following TDD.

Even on side projects, I often use TDD as a form of documentation. It means that if I do not work on the project for multiple months, the tests help me jump straight back in.

Index

A

adapter layer 36
adapter pattern 121
Advanced Messaging Queuing Protocol
     (AMQP) protocol 139
aggregate pattern 53
  order 53
  team 54
  wallet 54
aggregates 53, 54
  beyond single bounded context 57
  designing 56
  discovering 55
Alpha 3 ISO-3166 format 116
Amazon Web Services (AWS) 134
anemic models 45-49
anti-corruption layer 36-38, 121-124
Apache Software Foundation (ASF) 145
application services 69-74

B

behaviour-driven development
     (BDD) 174-176
Big Blue Book 6
binary serialization 30

black-box testing 154
bounded context 20-22
  anti-corruption layer 36-38
  Open Host Service 22-24
  published language 24, 25
buf
  gRPC for Go with 32-35
  reference link 32

C

CAP theorem 135-137
Cassandra 136, 137
charges, creating in Stripe
  reference link 97
CoffeeCo system
  CoffeeBux, paying with 98-101
  infrastructure service, adding for
     payment handling 96, 97
  product repository, implementing 93-95
  scene, setting 81, 82
  service, extending 108
  store-specific discounts, adding 102-108
  working with 83-93
Command Query Responsibility
     Segregation (CQRS) 8, 64, 137-139
continuous integration (CI) 30

create, read, update, delete (CRUD) 9
Cucumber
   reference link 174

D

databases 135-137
DDD scorecard 9
distributed system 134, 135
   characteristics 134, 135
   failure, dealing with 141
distributed system patterns 137
   CQRS 137-139
   EDA 139-141
domain 14, 16
domain-driven design (DDD) 13
   adoption 7, 8
   applying, to monolithic application 109
   history 3-5
   pillars 6
   scene, setting 14
   strategic design 7
   tactical design 7
   ubiquitous language 6
   using, scenarios 9, 10
domain events 140
domain model 7
domain services 66-68

E

entities
   example 42-44
   warning 45
   working with 42
entity factories 63
event 139
event-driven architecture (EDA) 139-141

F

factory pattern 60-63
   entity factories 63

G

Gang of Four (GoF) 5
   behavioral patterns 6
   creational patterns 5
   structural patterns 6
Gherkin
   reference link 174
Golang
   repository pattern, implementing 63-66
GORM 49
   URL 49
gRPC 30-32
   for Go using buf 32-35
   selecting 35
gRPC endpoints
   reference link 35

H

human resources (HR) 4

I

identifiers
   generating 44, 45
input and output (I/O) events 139
International Business Machines
   Corporation (IBM) 8
International Organization for
   Standardization (ISO) 116
ISO-8601 format 116

J

Java 4

K

Kafka 145, 146
   challenge 146

M

message bus 145
   Kafka 145, 146
   NATS 148, 149
   RabbitMQ 146-148
microservices 112
   anti-corruption layer 121-124
   benefits 113
   characteristics 113
   company, adopting 114
   drawbacks 113, 114
   recommendation system, building 116-121
   scene, setting 114-116
   service, exposing via open
      host service 124-131
minimum viable product (MVP) 82
Mongo 135
monolithic application/monolith 80
   advantages 80
   building, with domain-driven
      design principles 81
   disadvantages 81
   domain-driven design (DDD),
      applying to 109

N

Neural Autonomic Transport
   System (NATS) 148, 149

O

object-oriented design (OOD) 4
object-oriented (OO) code 4
object-oriented (OO) languages 138
object-relational mappings (ORMs) 49
OOD patterns 5
OO programming (OOP) 4
OpenAPI 25-30
   selecting 35
Open Host Service 22-24
service, exposing via 124-131

P

partnership team 114
payments domain 16
protobuf 31
published language 24, 25
   gRPC 30-32
   OpenAPI 25-30

R

RabbitMQ 146-148
   disadvantages 148
recommendations team 114
Remote Procedure Call (RPC) 23, 112
repositories 63
repository layer 64
repository pattern
   implementing, in Golang 63-66

S

saga pattern 142-145
services 66
  application services 69-74
  domain services 66-68
single point of failure (SPOF) 136
Square
  reference link 98
sub-domains 16
subscriptions domain 16
Swagger 25
Swagger Editor
  reference link 27

T

test-driven development (TDD) 152
  code, writing to pass test 153, 156-161
  fail test, running 153-156
  refactoring 153, 162-173
  test, adding 152-155
  test, rerunning 153
ticket
  for user behaviors 153
two-phase commit (2PC) 141, 142
  completion phase 141
  preparation phase 141

U

ubiquitous language 16, 17
  benefits 17-20
  capture, ensuring 20
  warning on application 20
unique identifier (UID) 139
universally unique identifiers (UUIDs) 44
user interface (UI) 70

V

value objects 53
  working with 49-53

`Packt.com`

Subscribe to our online digital library for full access to over 7,000 books and videos, as well as industry leading tools to help you plan your personal development and advance your career. For more information, please visit our website.

Why subscribe?

- Spend less time learning and more time coding with practical eBooks and Videos from over 4,000 industry professionals

- Improve your learning with Skill Plans built especially for you

- Get a free eBook or video every month

- Fully searchable for easy access to vital information

- Copy and paste, print, and bookmark content

Did you know that Packt offers eBook versions of every book published, with PDF and ePub files available? You can upgrade to the eBook version at `packt.com` and as a print book customer, you are entitled to a discount on the eBook copy. Get in touch with us at `customercare@packtpub.com` for more details.

At `www.packt.com`, you can also read a collection of free technical articles, sign up for a range of free newsletters, and receive exclusive discounts and offers on Packt books and eBooks.

Other Books You May Enjoy

If you enjoyed this book, you may be interested in these other books by Packt:

Event-Driven Architecture in Golang

Michael Stack

ISBN: 978-1-80323-801-2

- Understand different event-driven patterns and best practices
- Plan and design your software architecture with ease
- Track changes and updates effectively using event sourcing
- Test and deploy your sample software application with ease
- Monitor and improve the performance of your software architecture

Practical Microservices with Dapr and .NET - Second Edition

Davide Bedin

ISBN: 978-1-80324-812-7

- Use Dapr to create services, invoking them directly and via pub/sub
- Discover best practices for working with microservice architectures
- Leverage the actor model to orchestrate data and behavior
- Expose API built with Dapr applications via NGINX and Azure API Management
- Use Azure Kubernetes Service to deploy a sample application
- Monitor Dapr applications using Zipkin, Prometheus, and Grafana
- Scale and load test Dapr applications on Kubernetes
- Get to grips with Azure Container Apps as you combine Dapr with a serverless platform

Packt is searching for authors like you

If you're interested in becoming an author for Packt, please visit `authors.packtpub.com` and apply today. We have worked with thousands of developers and tech professionals, just like you, to help them share their insight with the global tech community. You can make a general application, apply for a specific hot topic that we are recruiting an author for, or submit your own idea.

Share Your Thoughts

Now you've finished *Domain-Driven Design with Golang*, we'd love to hear your thoughts! Scan the QR code below to go straight to the Amazon review page for this book and share your feedback or leave a review on the site that you purchased it from.

`https://packt.link/r/1804613452`

Your review is important to us and the tech community and will help us make sure we're delivering excellent quality content.

Download a free PDF copy of this book

Thanks for purchasing this book!

Do you like to read on the go but are unable to carry your print books everywhere?

Is your eBook purchase not compatible with the device of your choice?

Don't worry, now with every Packt book you get a DRM-free PDF version of that book at no cost.

Read anywhere, any place, on any device. Search, copy, and paste code from your favorite technical books directly into your application.

The perks don't stop there, you can get exclusive access to discounts, newsletters, and great free content in your inbox daily

Follow these simple steps to get the benefits:

1. Scan the QR code or visit the link below

https://packt.link/free-ebook/9781804613450

2. Submit your proof of purchase
3. That's it! We'll send your free PDF and other benefits to your email directly

Ingram Content Group UK Ltd.
Milton Keynes UK
UKHW031940090523
421483UK00007B/110